For Mrs. Eileen and Mrs. Coleen
who taught me everything I know about Irish Dancing

Copyright © 2014 by Jacqueline Mullins.

Library of Congress Control Number: 2014911812
ISBN: Hardcover   978-1-4990-4324-2
       Softcover   978-1-4990-4323-5
       eBook   978-1-4990-4325-9

All rights reserved. No part of this book may be reproduced or transmitted in any form or by any means, electronic or mechanical, including photocopying, recording, or by any information storage and retrieval system, without permission in writing from the copyright owner.

Any people depicted in stock imagery provided by Thinkstock are models, and such images are being used for illustrative purposes only.
Certain stock imagery © Thinkstock.

This book was printed in the United States of America.

Rev. date: 08/18/2014

To order additional copies of this book, contact:
Xlibris LLC
1-888-795-4274
www.Xlibris.com
Orders@Xlibris.com

Contents

Chapter 1.	Drills and an Accident	1
Chapter 2.	Are We There Yet?	6
Chapter 3.	Water Please and *Nothing* Extra!	8
Chapter 4.	Lily	11
Chapter 5.	The Return of the Witch	13
Chapter 6.	Big News!	17
Chapter 7.	Early Morning Practice!	21
Chapter 8.	Who's Snooping?	26
Chapter 9.	Hornpipes	32
Chapter 10.	Don't Worry, Nothing Will Happen!	38
Chapter 11.	What Is That Noise?	42
Chapter 12.	What Happened?	45
Chapter 13.	What Happened, Part 2	47
Chapter 14.	Daisy Dances	52
Chapter 15.	Recalls	55
Chapter 16.	Calie McDaniel	59
Chapter 17.	Set Dances	64
Chapter 18.	Patrick	67
Chapter 19.	Awards	71
Chapter 20.	U8 Solo's Wake-Up Call	76
Chapter 21.	Proof	82
Chapter 22.	Game Plan	86
Chapter 23.	Sardines	91
Chapter 24.	Locked	95
Chapter 25.	Justice	99

Chapter 1

Drills and an Accident

"Mom, I told you, I have the step down already," I say to my mom, Annabelle, who is the teacher and owner (along with her sister) of Mullins School of Irish Dance.

"Let's see it then," says Mrs. Annabelle—at least that's what all her students call her. Her eyes resemble the light blue walls that surround the studio (besides the mirrors of course).

It's funny. I know the floorboards so well that if you tell me to point to the fifth little nick in the thirtieth panel, I can do it with my eyes closed. That's how much time I spend practicing and just sitting here.

I start on my new reel step:

One two-step, step and double knee leap over, and double-jump point hop back switch, switch, and right two whip and left two spring, and one two step step hop down twirl whip. "Ow!" I cry out as I fall out of my twirl.

"Oh my gosh, honey! Are you okay?"
"No, I can't even move it!" I bawl.
"Let me help you up."
"No, I'll get up myself!"

When I try to stand up, I instantly fall back down. My right ankle is now the size of an orange!

"We have some good news though, you were right. You do have the step down," she exclaims trying to be funny, which usually cheers me up. Today, however, it isn't working.

"Now it feels like needles!" I sob with my head pressed against my knees.

"Let me help you up."

"Fine," I say, still crying.

"I'm going to take *you* to the hospital right now!"

-♫♫♫-

While the doctor is examining the x-ray, I tell myself, *it can't be broken, it just can't be broken.* The pain has sort of subsided (barely [it really hasn't gotten better]). The thing that I am most worried about is Nationals. It is next weekend. If it is sprained or broken, that means I will have to miss it.

"Well, that doesn't look very good,." The doctor pouts while *still* looking at the x-ray. "You are going to need crutches and a cast for roughly three months at *least*," he says, emphasizing *least*.

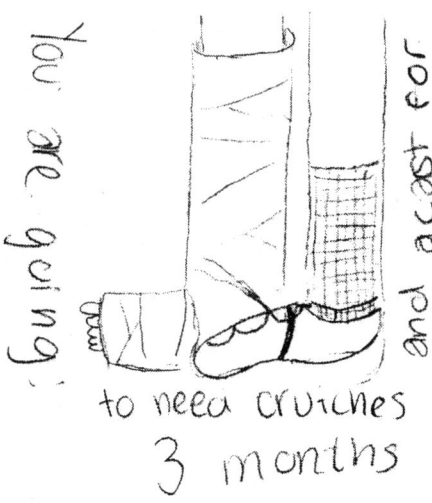

"Okay," says my mom solemnly.

"Wait, I have to be on crutches and in a cast for three months? That's impossible! Nationals are next weekend!" I say out loud now.

"I'm sorry, but you're just going to have to miss it," he says pitifully.

"All right, Ginny, settle down."

"I'm going to go and get to cloth for your cast. It's not plaster yet," the doctor says.

I don't respond.

He comes back with five rolls of cloth and four rolls of fluffy cotton.

He wraps it around my leg, and he asks me if it is too tight. He also has the hot and hard thing that is a mold of my leg. The mold of my foot is really wet and warm, and the cotton is soft but that doesn't help the constant waves of pain that are bringing me close to tears all over again. I think that I am going to die.

We get into our car, and the first thing that I tell my mom is that my life is over. I can't possibly live for another week much less the rest of my life without going to *these Nationals*! Last year I got second! I was hoping to get first this year and to start a roll.

"Well, honey, you can't do everything," she says.

I am stunned. Is she seriously okay with this? Does she seriously think that *this* is what is supposed to happen? I can't believe this! Oh well, that's the last time that I'll tell her about something that's on my mind!

-♪♪♪-

"Why can't I go, Mom? Please, please, please, please, please, and please!"

"Fine, you can come but you may not participate. This would've been your last dance class, so everybody will be wondering what happened."

"Fine!"

"But you know, Ginny, if I see you on the stage or even without your crutches on, you won't go to Nationals, not even to watch!"

"No way," I say.

"Yes way," she replies with the same amount of sass. I thought that being sassy was my thing!

-♫♫♫-

"Oh . . . my . . . gosh! What happened?" asks Lanie, one of my best friends.

"Oh, I broke four parts of my ankle," I say to Lanie, Madge, and Alice, my three best friends.

"That sucks," says Alice.

"Yeah," I say.

"Well, at least you did Nationals last year as a U11 [which was my age group. That means that now I am U12]," says Madge.

"I guess," I say.

Another girl from our dance class comes up to me. "Ginny, what happened?"

"Oh, I broke—"

"Sorry, tell me later. Come on, Lanie, it's our turn to dance!" she urges Lanie.

Her name is Abby. She can't sit still for more than five seconds. I wonder sometimes how she sleeps!

-♫♫♫-

When class is over, my mom takes me to some special doctor's office to have my leg actually wrapped in a physical *plaster* cast. What I don't understand is, why couldn't they just do that at the hospital? It sure would save people a lot of time and money!

We wait for an extra fifteen minutes, and when the nurse finally comes out, it is way past dinnertime and I am famished!

She leads us into the first room on the left, and then we wait for another ten minutes before the cast doctor or whatever comes in.

"Tell me if anything hurts, okay, dear?" he says.

The man is aging with gray hair, wrinkles, and a gray mustache. His name is Dr. Hendricks. He starts to unwrap the cotton cast, and when he finishes, he asks me if we want to keep any of it. I shake my head. I want that stuff as far away from me as possible! Also, I am in a bad mood because when he takes of the cast, my foot kills!

Then he starts wrapping some more cotton around my leg. It is nice and soft against my red and swollen leg. Next, he starts to get out the different colors that he had for the plaster casts. There is orange, green, dark blue, black, red, white, or pink. I choose orange—my favorite color! He wraps it around my leg already covered with cotton. The cast goes up to just under my knee. It also takes a couple of minutes to dry, so I sit there in dead silence, glaring at anyone (even the doctor) who tries to start up a conversation. When the cast finally dries, it was time to go back home. Finally, I can go up to my room and sulk!

A while later my parents make me come downstairs.

I make it to the stairs and wonder how I am going to get down. Well, it is going to have to be the same way I got up—by sliding on my bottom. I finally make it down with my crutches and hobble into the kitchen. On the table I see my all-time favorite dessert—Bananas Foster! Incredible!

"Thank you so much," I say, smiling. I guess good stuff does come out of a broken leg!

"We figured that you would like it," my dad laughs.

"You're right," I say and then devour it.

Chapter 2

Are We There Yet?

"When are we going to be there?" I ask my mom while watching *McKenna Shoots for the Stars* for the tenth time in twelve hours. I am at the part where she wins the regional competition . . . again. *Stupid fairytale endings!*

"We are going to be there in three hours," says my mom.

"Why does nationals have to be in Boston? Why can't it be in Wisconsin or somewhere close like that?" I ask.

"Believe me, honey, if it were up to me, I'd make it in our studio!"

"Mom, my foot hurts," I complain after a long awkward silence.

"Then I'll give you an aspirin," she replies while reaching into her purse.

"No! Have you ever tasted one of those? It tastes like dog poo!" I exclaim.

"Well, what else am I supposed to do?"

"Give me the ice pack, if you brought it."

"Honey, an ice pack isn't going to help a leg with plaster wrapped in it."

"Fine," I say stubbornly.

"I can still give you an aspirin."

"No, I'll wait until we get there. Oh wait, if we had taken a plane, I guess that we would've been there already!" I snap.

"Ginny Rose Mullins, you stop complaining right now or I'll call your Aunt Samantha and bring you to her house and you will stay there until nationals is over with. Do you understand? You know how much stress I am under right now? Probably not, but stop complaining and read a book. Aunt Jackie's kids will be there before we will, so I will call Aunt Jackie right now to see if I can drop you off when we get there so I can unpack. Got it?"

"Sure."

"Good," says my mom, "now read, and turn that movie off!"

I might've forgotten to mention that my aunt Jackie is always at any competition first. She has never been beat to one, so that is why my mom said she would be there first. She also said this because she sees her sister's car right in front of hers!

Chapter 3

Water Please and *Nothing* Extra!

"Finally we're here!" I say. "Sixteen and a half hours in a car with only two bathroom breaks can give you really bad neck cramp!" I say.

"Yeah," says my mom.

The hotel has polished, shiny white marble pillars. The tile floors are a tan color, and I can't help staring at the pattern that it makes. The front desks are brown oak wood, and the marble counter on top of them is also shiny. Something about this place is too new and too perfect.

8

I think that this is the sort of place that you don't want to be wandering around in its basement alone. It is the type of place where you need to watch your back. All the workers seem nice except for the one that we are waiting in line for. It is like she is the one casting the evil spell on the rest of the place.

"Here's your room key," says the lady behind the desk, with a Southern accent. "Oh no, Ginny, what happened to your poor foot?"

"Oh, I broke it," I say. But how the heck does she know my name? I didn't think anyone had used it after we entered the hotel.

"Okay, let's go, honey," says my mom, oblivious to the fact that the lady at the check-in counter just used my real name when she should have no idea who I am and what my name is . . . Very strange!

The lady behind the desk waves with an overly friendly smile that makes me even more confused, but I wave back with an equally fake smile. Her smile is also suspicious. It is a smile that I see *a lot* from my mom, but I am a little worried seeing it from another adult. I decide to keep a careful watch on her.

-♪♪♪-

"So how's your foot in a cast?" asks my cousin Daisy, who looks at me scornfully because I'm not doing Nationals with her.

"Fine," I say while going to sit down on a stool.

Daisy and I are best friends, but we are cousins, so technically it doesn't count.

"All right, let's get started," says my aunt Jackie to all the dancers in the practice room that the Mullins School of Irish Dance has reserved for the week.

The room has pale yellow walls that seriously needed to be repainted. The wooden floors are freshly sanded, dry, and easy to dance on. There are little tables in every corner (one of them has the music player on it), and chairs have been placed around the rest of the perimeter of the room.

"See you, Ginny. Call me on my cell if you need me. I'll be unpacking in our room," says my mom.

"Bye."

While I sulk and pitifully watch the other dancers perform, all the shame inside me causes my foot to start hurting (I really don't know why), so I decide to get a glass of water. I get my crutches and tell my aunt Jackie that I will be right back.

When I go to the front desk to ask for some water, I come face to face with Leslie, the lady who gave me the room keys.

I boldly "crutch" up and say, "May I have a glass of water?"

"Sure, ice or no ice?" asks the lady.

"Ice please," I say.

The lady smiles that fake, evil smile. She turns and leaves to get the water. I really don't have a good feeling about this woman. I wonder if I am acting too prim and proper, but that is how my mom has always told me to talk, so there won't be any changing habits now!

When the lady returns, I smile and say, "Thank you," while trying to figure out how to use crutches and hold my freezing cold water at the same time.

"Would you like some help with that?" the lady asks with her Southern sweetie-pie voice that reminded me of that Disney fairy Rosetta.

"No thanks," I say, "I'll be fine."

"Are you sure?" she asks. "I wouldn't want a precious angel like you getting lost."

"No really, our practice room is right around the corner."

I truly can use some help, but there is no way that I will ask *her* to help me. Instead I wave with the hand that isn't holding the freezing water and turn to go.

"Okay, suit yourself," She shrugs.

While I walk away, I can see out of the corner of my eye that she is talking to another lady behind the tall wooden desk and pointing at me. I remind myself to come up with a nickname for the lady really soon.

Chapter 4

Lily

When I finally get back to the room five minutes later, Daisy is dancing, so I sit down and watch.

Bang and a rally knock heel, bang, toe, and a rally bang rally step high click and bang toe. Click, click and toe hop spin bang and a rally hop back tip and knock and bang, toe left 1, 2, 3 tip and bang twirl, and a rally bang rally toe and a heel and a rally hop back brush, brush toe, toe, toe, and a rally toe rally hop back (toe).

I sing softly in my head while Daisy does her steps. Daisy and I do the same steps, so I know them well.

Daisy's little sister, Lily, all of a sudden jumps on my lap, which makes me grunt really loud. I stare at Lily, but she just laughs at me and thinks it is really funny, so I have to crack a smile myself. Lily is seven, and she is doing solos for Oireachtas later this year but she is acting like it is tomorrow. (She is really excited to be doing solos for the first time in her life!) Lily is the best dancer in her age group, and she can dance like a U9 even though she is a U7. She has really high expectations for Oireachtas. I know she will do great!

"I like you," says Lily.

"Why thank you. I like you too," I say.

"So does that mean I can play on your phone?"

"Maybe next time," I say.

"Pretty, pretty please with a cherry on top! I won't ask for any icebreakers for a whole week!" They are her very favorite, and every dance class when she is there, she always asks me to get one from my dance bag.

"Fine," I say. I mean, how can I refuse her sweet little smile? I pull it out of my bag and tell her, "I need it back in ten minutes, okay?"

It is hard to keep the phones and iPads charged for the whole day, and I know Lily will play on it for hours if I don't tell her no.

"Okay," she says while she crosses her heart.

When I look outside the entryway, I see the front desk lady (a.k.a. the Witch, which is the new nickname I just came up with for her). When the Witch sees me looking at her, she walks toward my aunt like nothing happened. She talks to her for a little bit, nods, and smiles her usual fake smile that apparently I am the only one noticing is fake. I am wondering what she wants, but I have been too far away to overhear anything of the conversation!

Chapter 5

The Return of the Witch

"Hi, Mom," I say as I make my way into our hotel room.

It has two twin beds, a queen-size sofa, a queen-size bathroom, and a lot of space. (It *would've* been perfect for practicing steps.)

"Hey, hon, I'm just finishing up here. So how do you like the room?" she asks.

"It's great," I say.

I decide not to tell her about the Witch. It's not like she will believe *me* anyway.

"In about an hour we are going to go down to the practice rooms for the U8 practice. Okay?"

"Okay."

-♪♪♪-

"*Oh no!* Ginny, what happened to your foot?" asks Paige, a U8.

"Oh, I broke it," I say while wondering, *How many times do I have to say this?*

"How did you break it?" asks Maggie, Paige's twin sister and another U8.

"I was dancing with my mom and I twirled, and I tripped, and I fell."

"So how long are you going to have your cast on?" implores Paige.

"Three months."

"That's a long time," says Maggie.

"Yeah," says Paige.

"So do you want to go and get some water with me?" Maggie asks.

"Didn't you bring some of your own?" I question.

"I forgot."

"Okay, well, do you want some too, Paige?"

"Sure, I'll go and tell your mom that we'll be right back."

"Okay, Maggie and I will be waiting outside the door."

-♩♩♩-

"Okay, let's go," I say.

"Do you know where you are going?" asks Paige.

"Yeah, it's right down the hall," I reply.

"So can I have an Ice Breaker?" asks Maggie.

"So sorry, Maggie, but I ran out because you and Lily kept on eating them all."

"Oh, sorry."

"Okay, we're here," I say.

"Oh, back *again*, I see. Would you like some lemonade, you cutie-pies?" asks the Witch.

"Can we, Ginny? Please!" begs Paige.

"No. Lemonade doesn't hydrate you, water does. So anyway, ice or no ice?"

"Ice please," they both say in unison while beaming up at the Witch with puppy-dog eyes.

"No problem, sunshines," she says while turning around to get some.

"Her smile and her eyes scare me." Maggie worries.

"Yeah, me too," says Paige.

"There's nothing to worry about. She seems nice," I say while thinking, *Finally somebody else notices how weird she acts!*

"Yeah, well, anyway, let's just get our water and get out of here!" says Paige.

The Witch returns.

"Here you go, darlings. Now would you like one too? I'm sorry I don't know your name. Would you care to tell me?"

"Sure my name is Alex."

L-I-E.

She turns around and goes and gets my water.

Wait a minute. At the front desk when my mom and I checked in, she said, "Oh no, Ginny, what happened to your foot?" Something's fishy and I will find out what it is. After all, why on earth would anybody look into what my name is?

"Why would you say that?" asks Maggie.

"Hello? Stranger danger!" I say.

"Oh, right," says Maggie.

"Let's get out of here!" Paige whines.

"Wait, I haven't gotten my water yet."

"Oh, right," says Paige.

"Here is your water with ice, sweet tart," says the Witch.

"How did you know that she wanted ice in her water, and why does it smell like cherry, with red drops in it?" asks Maggie.

"Don't drink it, Gin . . . I mean Alex!" screams Paige.

"Wait, why did you call her Gin? Her name is Alex, right?" asks the Witch.

"Ginny is my twin's name. . . . We look a lot alike," I say, which is true. In my head I can totally picture my imaginary twin looking a lot like me!

"Oh, I see, and are these your sisters, too?" she asks with suspicion swiped across her face.

"No, but we dance at the same school and they are my second cousins," I say.

"Well, I see, does your sister have crutches too?"

"Yeah, actually permanently—she's disabled."

"I see. I'm so sorry. Well, good luck on your competition, you two, and I hope your foot feels better soon."

"Thank you," we call back to her.

"Okay, guys, let's get out of here!"

"Twins?" Maggie and Paige say at the same time. "You are such a liar."

They turn and wave to the Witch and give their true fake smile simultaneously. One thing about us Irish dancers is that we are really good at faking smiles or looking really happy on command. I think it is because we are so used to putting on a poker face when we get up on the stage that we just put on that smile whether nervous or anxious. Nobody can tell what emotions we are going through when we start to dance.

Chapter 6

Big News!

"Ginny, call your dad tonight." commands my mom.
"Okay, Mom, I will do it right now." I say.
While I dial my dad's number on my cell phone, I think about something. Why did my water smell like cherries, and why did it have drops of red liquid in it? I put that thought to the side and press the Call button.
"Hi, Dad."
"Hi, Ginny, how's your foot feeling?"

"Fine."

"How's the old woman [Mom] doing?"

"Good, it's going to be a long day tomorrow."

"That's nice, honey," he says, sounding really distracted. "Can I speak to your mom for a quick second?"

"Sure."

Well, that's what I call a real blow-off. He normally keeps a conversation going for ages.

"Good night."

"Good night, Ginny."

I give the phone to my mom, and she goes in the bathroom to talk, which makes me wonder why dad was in such a hurry to get mom on the line. My suspicion grows even bigger when she turns on the shower, so I can't hear anything she is saying. Whatever it is, I will find out sooner or later!

When my mom finally comes out from the bathroom, I look at her with real suspicious eyes and say, "So what's so secret I can't hear about it?"

"Well, hon, now that I have to tell you. . . . I have some good and some bad news. The bad news is that your dad and I have been keeping a pretty big secret from you, your sister, and your brother for four months, and the good news is that we are having . . . um . . . a baby in five months. The baby will be born right before Oireachtas in the fall."

"Wow, so that is why you are getting so fat. I thought you just ate too much. Wait, you knew this for four months and didn't even tell me? 'Cause as far as I know, it takes nine months to have a baby. Right?"

"Yes, Ginny. We just wanted to be sure so in case something happened, you wouldn't be disappointed."

"Wait, is it a boy or a girl?" I ask, curiosity taking over from feeling hurt that they hadn't shared the important information with me. I mean, I am part of this family . . . right?

"We're not sure yet. We want it to be a surprise," she says while looking away.

Okay, now I am getting pretty excited.

"But why did Dad want to talk to you so much?"

"He just wanted to say that the doctor had called with some results and the baby was looking nice and healthy, but I still have to take it real easy."

"Well, that should be no problem being here at nationals," I say sarcastically.

My mom is always *super* stressed and totally hectic when any big competition is going on.

"I know, but I try to sit down as much as possible and not walk too much."

"Have you told Charlie or Bella yet?" I ask. Charlie and Bella are my younger siblings.

"No, actually, I will be telling them when we get back."

"Why again isn't Bella here?"

"Ginny, for the last time, she is three and is way too young to be dancing at Nationals."

I go out to the bathroom to get ready for bedtime and call out to my mom, "You better not have decided on a name for my baby brother or sister. . . . I think I deserve to have a say in the name picking since I was kept in the dark for so long!" I mean, that is only fair . . . right? I brush my teeth, wash my hands and my face, and take out my contact lenses.

There is still one thing that is bothering me though. Why was the red liquid in my water? Did the Witch put it there on purpose, and if that is the case, *why*? I am just about ready to ask my mom what she thinks about it all, but think better of it. The last thing she needs is more to worry about, with the baby and all. I better just wait for tomorrow and discuss it with Madge, Alice, Daisy, and Lanie. I decide to forget about it for tonight, and instead I started to think of cute names I like for my little baby brother or sister.

"Hey, honey, is your foot hurting? I can always give you an aspirin."

"Okay, I'll take it," I say with a vile taste already growing in my mouth.

"Okay, it's at the table at the foot of my bed."

I look at the grape-tasting pill. I start to feel like I am going to throw up, but I take it anyway. All the water that I was holding in my bottle is gone in ten seconds (a new personal record, and it was a small bottle!).

I hop into bed, say a prayer for all the Mullins School of Irish Dance dancers, and clutch my favorite stuffed animal, Lambie. About three seconds later, I am sound asleep.

Chapter 7

Early Morning Practice!

Beep, beep, beep, beep, beep, beep! My mom slams her hand on top of the Snooze bar. I lay on top of the twin-size bed that I had claimed when I walked into the room yesterday and instantly feel my foot. It hurts. I get out of bed and hobble to the bathroom where the grape-flavored kids' aspirins are.

Instant relief, the package doesn't lie—*not*!

"Mom, what time do the U12 solo's start?"

"In three hours."

"So at eight thirty?"

"Yes."

"It's five thirty, did I seriously have to get up this early? I am just saying!"

"Well, I have to be down there at the latest by six thirty for practices. We have to eat before, and practices start at seven."

"What, why?"

"Ask your aunt."

I don't reply. Getting up at five thirty makes absolutely *no* sense!

I brush my teeth, French-braid my hair, comb my hair, put contacts in my eyes, and wash my face, and then I French-braid my hair again.

It is six when we leave for the elevators. We meet Alice, Madge, and Lanie with their moms at the lobby. Apparently they had a makeup session and did each other's makeup and wigs. They did it *without me*! Anyway, they have their wigs and makeup and practice clothes on, and all of them are half-asleep.

I ask my mom if I can tell them about her being pregnant. She says yes, so I do. Of course their moms probably already know.

"Guess what," I say to my friends.

"What?" they all answer at the exact same time.

"My mom is having a baby," I exclaim.

"Oh . . . my . . . gosh. . . . Really?" asks Alice.

"Yeah," I say.

"Boy or girl?" asks Lanie.

"We don't know. My parents want a surprise."

"Oh," they all say, kind of disappointed.

"The baby is going to be born five days before the Oireachtas," I say proudly.

"Wait, so you've known for four months and you haven't said a thing?" asks Madge with a big frown on her face, doing the math in her head, as she is a mathematician. Madge has pale skin and *thick* dark brown hair. She has sea green eyes, a few freckles, and pale pink lips.

"Actually," I say, staring at my mom, who smiles back at me really cheesily, "I found out yesterday, so if you feel left outside the information flow, how do you think I feel?"

Everyone is quiet. Good, I like being on top of the food chain.

"Wow," says Alice.

She has long and wavy blond hair. She has pale skin and perfect strawberry lips. She also has very bright blue eyes. They are the kind that you would see in a magazine. If you watch the original *Alice in Wonderland*, you will think that the real Alice (the one who is standing right next to me) came straight out of the movie . . . That is exactly why she is named Alice! She is the sassy but kind one of us. She was probably going to get a boyfriend first. She is a little taller than the rest of us.

Lanie, Alice, and Madge are Daisy's friends too, but she has others that came before them say they were to be written down on a list numbered best friends and down. We are all in the same class. Well, Madge, Alice, Lanie, and I. In kindergarten, Daisy and I were *really* big troublemakers. We haven't been in the same class since. Figures. Even though we are split, we will never really be, well, split. B-F-F-L!

Lanie on the other hand was the short and quiet one who always seems to be in the middle of a good part in a book. At Irish Dance though, she isn't as quiet and shy. In fact, she can bounce the highest when she wants to. She is also very athletic and good at sports. If she ever tried in gym class instead of reading, she would be at an A+++!

Lanie has short, messy, curly red hair and a completely freckled face. She has strawberry lips and dark blue/gray eyes. Lanie has an average height.

I have a lighter brown mixed with a little orange and blond hair, a tiny bit of freckles on my nose, greenish eyes, and olive skin. I am pretty short.

The Witch is at the front desk again today. I am seriously considering going up to her to check her pockets and see if she has hidden any knives or magic wands and, if she has any wands, make my foot heal. But that is a topic that I still will have to consider.

"Okay, guys, let's start practicing," says my mom.

Daisy arrives five minutes later. She is clearly going to need to eat some pixie sticks or energy bars before she performs. She literally collapses into a chair and puts on her soft shoes with less energy than a turtle. Literally! Daisy has thick wavy dark brown hair and perfect pale skin and rosy cheeks. She is short like me. We get it from our mom's side.

I sit down beside her and say, "Hey, Daisy, sleep well?"

"No," she says, really gloomy. "Can you tell? I kept on having this dream that while I was dancing my set dance, I would trip and fall like you and break my foot or something like that. Then I would get last place for recalls, I can't have that, Ginny. It would ruin me," she says really dramatically.

I snap my fingers by her face and say, "Snap out of it, Daisy. It was just a bad dream. You are the best dancer here, so get it out of your head and focus on today." I snap my fingers again for even better effect. "But don't tell Alice, Lanie, and Madge I said that. I will bet you fifty dollars that it won't happen."

"Okay, I guess so, but if my dream comes true, you owe me fifty dollars. Okay?" She looks at me with a smooth smile, and I know that not only is she going to try and win, but she is also determined to beat her dream.

"Okay," I say.

Like a fortune-teller, when Daisy is dancing, she fell on her ankle. It is a minor twist, but it would make her dance even harder and stop her from holding back.

All of a sudden my mom clamps her hand over her mouth and runs out of the practice room. Everyone turns to where she was standing and looks around, wondering what is wrong. I wonder where she is heading, but then it his me—the bathroom! Morning sickness! I always wondered why she took so long in the bathroom these days!

While my mom is in the bathroom, my aunt takes over the practices.

"Don't dance your hearts out, guys. . . . Conserve your energy," says my aunt.

Meanwhile, more and more U12s show up until all of them are there, except my mom, who is the only one missing. I decide to go look for her. After all, there is only one bathroom on the lobby floor. I tell my aunt that I am going to the washroom and sneak out of there as much as you can leave quietly and unseen when you have crutches and always bang into things.

While I crutch to the bathroom, I pass a bunch of solo Irish dancers. They are all ready to dance in their wigs, makeup, and beautiful dresses. Oh, by the way, I *love* Irish dance dresses, so I have to check out their outfits. You can always tell who is the hotshot dancer in a crowd; they just stick out. Their dresses are the newest styles, and they are totally intense and anxious because they have so much pressure on them. If they did really well last year, they want to do even better this year or keep their title, which is really tough because the competition is so hard. There is always someone that practices more than you and just wants that trophy even more.

Anyway, I search through all the pretty dresses but see no Mom anywhere. As I make my way into the bathroom, I spot her. Her hair is all messed up and her face is greenish. She is splashing water on her face and smiles when she sees me. I smile back and go over to the sink.

"How come you were here for such a long time?" I ask, trying to sound like I seriously don't know.

"Because of stupid morning sickness, I had it when I had—" she says without finishing.

"Yeah, yeah, okay," I interrupt, "let's not get all mushy gushy."

"Okay," she says sarcastically while drying her hands.

When she is done, we head back together.

Chapter 8

Who's Snooping?

While my mom and I walk back, she trips on her very high heels and falls to the ground.

"Shoot!" she says while fighting back tears.

What do you know, the Witch magically appears, running over to help her. I mean, that is really nice of her and all, so maybe I am wrong about her all along. I start to feel bad about all the bad thoughts I have about her.

"Oh my, are you all right?" she says totally sincerely.

"Yes, I'm fine," says my mom while looking at her foot, which is all red and puffy in her black shiny high heels, "but I guess I won't be wearing these heels for a while."

"Would you like to see the emergency nurse?" she asks.

"No, I'll be all right. Thank you though."

"All right, bye now, and please let me know if I can be of any assistance. You might want to put some ice on that foot."

"Mom, are you okay?" I ask.

"I'll be fine," she snaps while carefully walking back to the practice room.

-♪♪♪-

"What on earth happened?" asks my aunt when she sees her sister's swollen foot.

"Oh, I tripped a little," says my mom.

"A little? Do you want some ice?" asks my aunt.

"Do you mind?"

"Not at all. Madge, come here. Will you get an ice pack for Mrs. Annabelle, and, Ginny, will you go to the room and get her gym shoes?"

"Sure," we say simultaneous.

"Ginny, here's our room key," says my mom.

"Okay, bye," I say and jump as fast as my crutches allowed me. I stop by the front desk and ask for a plastic bag so the shoes will be easier to carry once I get them.

I make my way to the elevator and press button 2 for the skywalk that leads you to the actual hotel instead of the convention center. When I get across it, I press the button 14 in that elevator. I hurry down the long winding hall and slide in the room key that lets me into room number 1411. When I unlock our door, I see that our bedroom has been cleaned. I always hate when total strangers go through our personal stuff.

I find her worn-out gym shoes and put them in the plastic bag when all of a sudden, I hear someone at our door. I quickly hide behind a big chair. I mean, aren't the staff always supposed to knock before they come into the rooms just in case the guests are in there? I just got my crutches hidden away when the door opens. My heart is beating so fast, I am sure whoever it is can hear me for sure.

I slowly peek out and I can't believe what I see. It is the Witch! I knew she isn't to be trusted. She is snooping around, and when she gets to my bag, which is on my bed, she goes through the whole bag. What is she doing? My heartbeat is for sure near a heart attack rate. What is she doing here in our room, going through all my stuff? She finally sees Lambie, my stuffed animal that I have had since I was a baby and has always slept in my arms every night. It is my dearest possession and I love it so much, and for sure would never be able to sleep without it . . . *ever*! She stares at it, smiles wickedly, and tries to stuff him under her navy blue blazer.

I don't know what came over me, but I jump out from my hiding place and scream at her.

"What are you doing?" Not waiting for an answer, I carry on, "Put Lambie down—*now*!"

She looks at me with a horrified expression. Totally stunned she drops Lambie on the floor.

"What . . . um . . . what are you doing up here?" she asks. "I thought you were downstairs with all the others?"

I quickly snatch Lambie up and hold him tightly.

"I came up here to get my mom's gym shoes," I say. "Why were you taking Lambie?"

"I, eh, I was going to get him cleaned for you."

She is a very skilled liar, but she is too used to having people believing her. That totally ruined it! I certainly am not falling for it.

"No, you weren't," I say. "You were going to steal him!"

"You silly child, why would I want to steal a child's stuffed animal away?" She laughs as she says it.

I have to admit that it is a good question. Why would an adult steal Lambie? It just doesn't make any sense.

"I don't know. Maybe the same reason you tried to poison me?" I shoot back.

"I don't know what you are talking about child."

She seems taken away. I finally made someone lost for words. That's one more thing that I can check off my bucket list.

I know she is lying. She literally has "LIAR" written across her face.

"Come with me," I command. She follows me to the elevator. When it arrives, we step inside and I press the button 2 for the skywalk.

We walk across the skywalk and then go down to the main floor of the convention center on another elevator.

"Wait," I say, "do you know what time it is?"

"Yeah, it is eight."

We step out of the elevator and make our way to the practice room, where everyone is getting ready to leave.

I bring the Witch straight to my mom and say, "Mom, I found this lady snooping around in our room."

"Oh, well that's not good, now is it?" my mom says while I think, *Thank goodness, somebody else is noticing how weird this lady is!*

"No, it's not," I say, staring at the Witch.

"Go and play with Daisy or whomever, while I straighten things out."

"Okay. Oh, and, Mom, here are your shoes," I say, sort of sad that I'm not allowed to be part of that conversation. I walk over to Daisy to tell her the latest developments about the Witch. She is wearing her new solo dress, and it looks smashing on her.

"Congrats on your new dress. It looks really cute on you. Do you love it?"

"I do. Now we can't blame the results on the look!"

I tell her everything about what happened in the room, and she can't believe it. We look over at my mom, who is in deep conversation with the Witch. It looks like they are just about done talking, and we are both dying to know what was said over there. I say to Daisy that I bet she filled my mom with lies about the whole thing, so my mom believes her. But I have to focus on Daisy since she has to get ready for her competition.

"Are you all stretched out and warmed up?" I ask her while thinking that we shouldn't be talking small talk. I should be giving her a pep talk or something so she can get all fired up before dancing.

"Yeah, I'm good. Hey do you have any M&M's?"

"Sure."

I reach into my bag and grab them, and as I hand them to her, I smell the distinct smell of skunk. It is a smell you can't misplace. Our old dog used to get skunked a lot, so I know the smell very well. It is the real deal, not the smell that folks give you to trick you. I can only think of one thing . . . I will never eat M&M's again, and then I pass out. The next moments are a blur. First I am getting M&M's all over me, then I see Daily kneeling over me shaking me back to reality, and then I am in my mom's arms, drifting away again.

-♪♪♪-

The first thing I think about when I wake up is the Witch and how she must have put skunk smell into the bag of M&M's, but how did she do that?

I am in a white room with bright lights shining on my eyes. A nurse is looking down at me and tells someone that I am awake.

"How are you feeling?" the nurse asks me.

"I'm okay," I reply and turn my head in her direction, which I shouldn't have done because a pain shoots through my head. She must have seen my expression and looks at me with concern. Then my mom walks up.

"When are Daisy, Lanie, Alice, and Madge dancing?" I ask, trying to ignore the pain in my foot and my head.

"Ten minutes," she replies.

"We need to get over there," I say, almost panicked.

"Hold on we've got plenty of time. The stage is right across the hall."

"Do you have a Motrin for my foot?" I partly lie.

I mean, my foot is hurting, but my head is worse. There is no way I am telling the nurse that otherwise she won't let me out of here.

"Sure, kiddo." She hands me a pill, and I take one before she even hands me the water.

"That was a bad fall for you. I had to get the girls behind the stage, that's why I was gone for five minutes."

"I'm okay," I say. "So, shall we?"

"Sure."

"By the way, how's your foot?" I ask when I see her limping.

"Fine."

L-I-E.

Chapter 9

Hornpipes

The stage room is really pretty. It has creamy white walls, tan carpeting on the floors, and a large stage toward the back.

In front of the stage, there are three tables, one for each of the judges. On top of each table are a lamp, a bowl of candy, and a pitcher of water.

I don't have time to admire the room long though because all of a sudden, Daisy jumps in front of me, almost knocking me over! *Thanks a lot, Daisy!* I think.

"Oh my gosh, are you okay?" she screams.

"Yeah, I'm fine!" I snap while finding my seat.

"So why did you pass out?" asks Alice.

"I don't know, I guess that I just didn't get enough sleep," I say—*total* L-I-E!

"Calling competitors 103 to 132 backstage. [Just so you know, first, they always start with the number 101. Second, they always draw a random number from a hat to see who goes first. I guess this time the number was 103.] . . . And please check in your number before you go backstage," says the lady behind the podium next to the stage.

"I better go, guys," says Lanie, who is number 106.

"Good luck, Lanie! I know you will do great!" I say, and as if on cue, so does everyone else.

Madge, Alice, and Daisy must know to not to ask me anything because their eyes are full of questions. They are just dying to hear what happened and why I passed out.

"I really like all your new dresses, guys."

I'm just not in the mood to explain what happened right now. This is about Lanie and her doing great up on stage, not me.

"Thanks," all three of them say.

"Ooh, ooh, there's Lanie." And we are all quiet and hold hands of pure excitement and nerves.

The easiest round (in my opinion) is the first. Hard shoes are like tap shoes. Then there are soft shoes, like ballet shoes, where you have to be very graceful and have total body control with pointed toes and fully outstretched legs. Your upper body is totally relaxed and doesn't move, and your hands are tucked away neatly at your side. Trust me, you are not relaxed, but it just has to look that way. You have high jumps and have to land on your tippy toes while looking totally smiley and pretending like it is the easiest thing in the world. Well, trust me, it is not! Anyway, Lanie is doing hard shoes first and looks good so far.

And bang and left, one, two, turn and bang, and a rally step high-click and bang heel step heal step heel step and bang and treble, treble, treble knock and a heel bang. Click, click and bang and 1, 2, 3 twirl rally bang, rally step and high-click and tip and toe tip and tip and toe tip and tip and toe treble and knock switch.

That is Lanie's first step on the right foot; imagine what the rest of her dance is like.

"That was good, she needs to stay on her toes more though," says my mom. She sees everything.

When she comes back, she runs into her mom's arms. She did really well.

"I told you that you would do great!" I say high-fiving her.

"Yeah, you were awesome!" says Alice.

"Yeah, okay, thanks," Lanie says in between large gasps of breath.

Lanie goes over to my mom to hear the verdict. You always want to hear what your teacher has to say. They will encourage you and make you feel good about the small mistakes you know you did. They won't sugarcoat it like your friends and your mom and dad might but will tell you the facts in a good and encouraging way.

My mom says, "You were fabulous, and it looked really good. I would have liked to see you higher on your toes a few times, but the judges won't take much off, so you are good. Well done, Lanie, now you can take a deep breath and be really proud of your performance."

She gives Lanie a hug and tells her to get some water and get ready for next round.

The only person that isn't congratulating Lanie is Daisy. She is sitting off to the side, looking all miserable and pale, which is really hard considering the amount of tanning lotion and bronzer she is wearing.

"Okay," I say, "what's wrong?"

"I don't know, it's just that I am so worried that I am going to fall," she mopes.

"Don't worry, you won't and if you do and you actually break your leg... then I will give you fifty dollars!" I smile at her and say, "Seriously, Daisy, stop worrying, re-duct-tape your shoes before going up on the stage and you will be just fine and stay firmly on the stage."

Duct-taping your hard shoes makes the bottoms of them less slippery. Dipping the shoes in coke or water helps you to make your soft shoes stickier so you don't slip so easily.

"I know. I'm just getting worried for no reason, but I just can't help it."

"Go congratulate Lanie. She did really well, don't you think?"

"Yeah, she did."

"Okay, so go on," I say and shove her off her seat.

"You did amazing, Lanie, you are definitely going to get top twenty!" Daisy says.

"Thanks . . . you guys are going to do great too," says Lanie.

"Calling competitors 134 to 153 backstage, and please check in with your competitor number in place before you go backstage," says the lady over the microphone that is next to the stage.

"Knock 'em dead," says Mrs. Jackie (Aunt Jackie for me) to Madge.

"Wait, I'm number 140," says Alice.

"Well, go, go, and go. You don't want to be late," says my mom while applying her ice pack.

"Mom, I got to go to the bathroom?" I say.

"Can you wait two minutes? I want you to see Madge, and then you can go and hurry on back to see Alice."

"Fine."

Only then do I notice that the lady next to the stage is the Witch!

"Mom, look, it's the lady who was snooping around in our room."

"That old bat, she said that she was going to wash our stuff, which is very strange because she isn't even a cleaning lady. I wonder if she takes such a personal interest in all the people in the hotel?" my mom asks ironically. "I just don't have the time or energy to take the matter up with hotel management."

"You don't like her either? Oh good! So I guess it's safe to tell you that she wants me killed, and she hates me!"

"I'm sure she doesn't want you dead!"

"Oh yeah, she so does. . . . She tried to poison me!"

"And may I ask how she tried that?"

"When Maggie, Paige, and I went to go and get some water, she came back with water, that I didn't want, and it had red drops of liquid in it, and it smelled like cherries."

I lie again, a little. It is beginning to become a bad habit and I will have to stop it. It's just that I want my mom to believe me. I am actually feeling parched just thinking about that water. I really need to get some.

"Okay, I see, but, honey, even though you have seen and read every single Harry Potter, spy, and adventure book there is, it doesn't mean that these things happen in real life. You have a vivid imagination, but I am sure there is a perfectly reasonable explanation behind why the water was reddish."

"No, there's not!"

"No? Anyway Madge is up." My mom's concentration is on Madge and I know she has forgotten all about my mysterious accounts and me.

While Madge is dancing, I softly sing out her steps and move my fingers like her footwork would look.

"That was beautiful," says my mom when Madge is all done.

When she comes back out to us, she jumps into her mom's arms and chugged a bottle of water in one long drag.

"How did I do?" she says while gasping for air and wiping off her lips and chin with her hand from all the water she drank.

"Excellent! I am so proud of you!" says my mom.

"Really? Thanks."

She has a happy glow about her and looks really proud of herself, which looks really cute.

"Guys, go put on your soft shoes. You don't want to be late for next round," I say.

"I'm going to the washroom really quick," I say.

"Okay, hurry up," says my mom.

"Okay," I say to my mom while racing off using my crutches. It is so crowded everywhere, so *racing* might not have been the right term, more like snailing behind a big lady that nobody can get around. These crutches are getting on my nerves.

Chapter 10

Don't Worry, Nothing Will Happen!

I swear, if I had the chance right now, these crutches would be in the Dumpster! I *finally* make it to the bathrooms and am amazed that there isn't a long line, with my luck and all. I hopped into the first stall that is open and do my business. When I get back out, I see that there are at least twenty people waiting in line. I can't believe my luck. I mean, how the tides have turned, and I hope it is a sign of how the rest of the afternoon would be.

Anyway, I go to wash my hands, and I see Daisy at one of the sinks looking pale and green in her face.

"Oh my gosh, what happened?" I ask her,

"I puked," she says, grossed out.

"Are you sick or is it nerves?" I question her.

"I don't know."

"Well, let's get you back, I bet your turn is coming up soon."

"Okay," she says, trying to look brave.

"What's your number?" I ask her.

"102," she says. "Oh, and Alice is dancing pretty soon."

"I know. That is why we need to get back quickly."

When we enter the stage room, we see Alice up on stage ready to dance. We literally push our way up to the stage area so we could see better. Somehow people must see our urgency and let us through, or maybe it is the beginning of my lucky afternoon?

And five, point six, and ready, get set and go . . .

And bang toe, and a 1, 2, 3, hit and down slice, and a 1, 2, 3 toe and down, toe and down and a high-click. And a rally, rally toe, and heel, heel bang, tip and bang treble, treble knock and a heel bang. And spring and bang and 1, 2, 3, twirl rally bang and a rally step and high click and a bang, bang, bang, brush, brush knock, and a rally, rally, rally back toe.

"That was good," I say to my mom after watching Alice's first step on her right foot.

"Yes, it was," she replies.

I see Daisy sitting away from us biting her nails. *What an overreactor!* I think to myself.

"Okay, I know what you are thinking about, but you shouldn't be thinking about that now. You should be thinking about that only if you recall!" I say.

"Ginny!"

"Okay, sorry, but anyway, you really shouldn't stress, you're lucky that you don't have to sit on the sidelines and watch."

"Yeah, I guess but—"

I cut her off before she could finish. "Hey, I'm not fortune-teller, but I am pretty sure that that won't happen!"

Personally, I am getting kind of irritated of how she is starting to think of only herself and no one else and acting a little bit selfish.

"Remember, before you go up, do that breathing exercise that your mom taught us—beaches in [you breathe in air and think of a calming beach] and storms out [you think of a type of storm and breathe out air].

"Yeah, okay," she says.

"Guys, look! It's Caroline McDaniels!" whispers Lanie before Daisy and I even sit down (she is number 127).

Caroline McDaniels is the best dancer in the whole world for our age group! Now that's saying something!

Now, I don't know her steps, but I can tell that what she just performed isn't that great. Well, in my eyes at least!

"Calling competitors numbers 154 to 183 backstage, and please check in your number before you go backstage, thank you," says the Witch.

"Anyone going?" asks my aunt while looking at all their numbers. They all shake their heads.

"I'll be right back," says my mom.

"Where are you going?" I ask her.

"To the bathroom!"

"Oh good. I have got to go too," I say even though I really don't.

I just want to see if her foot is actually okay.

"Okay, come on."

When my mom takes one step on her swollen foot, she winces. She won't be able to make it to the bathroom in an hour the way she looks, much less two minutes.

"Mom, should I call for that nurse?"

"No, you go to the bathroom."

But I'm not going to the bathroom; I am going to get that emergency nurse.

I whisper to my aunt, "I'm going to get that nurse for Mom."

She nods and says to my mom, "Why don't you sit for a while?"

My mom obeys, and I am off.

Chapter 11

What Is That Noise?

The closer I get to the doors, the louder it is, the shrieking. When I get into the halls, it is almost unbearable. As fast as I can with these stupid crutches, I "run" into the weird room with the bright lights.

When I shut the door, there is no sound at all. Weird. Then it hits me—soundproof walls! Duh!

"Um . . . excuse me," I ask to no one in particular.

"Yes, hold on," says a woman (I can tell by her voice) in the background.

The lady has short curly brown hair. She looks very old-fashioned. She has one of those little white caps on her head and was wearing a white blouse and a white skirt. Her name is Mable. She seems nice.

"Now what happened?" she asks.

She has a very Southern voice that reminds me automatically of the Witch. A cold shiver runs through me but I try to ignore it.

"Oh, I broke my leg."

"Now I can see that, but what are you doing here if you are already healing?" she asks.

"Um, my mom fell by the lobby earlier and now she can't really walk on her foot. She's a teacher and is going to be up and about all day, and tomorrow, and many days after that!" I say in one large breath. "She insists that she is fine, but I'm not buying it. What am I going to do?"

I see her eyes soften, and I know I can trust her.

"Now stop worrying, everything will be all right."

"But how . . . she can't even walk and it's disgusting."

"How?"

"Well, it's all red and puffy, and it looks like it's locked in one place, though I can't really tell," I explain.

I notice that she is jotting all this down on the notepad that she has been carrying the whole time, and before I could help it, I blurt out, "So are you going to help her or what?"

I quickly shut myself up and stare at the green and white tiles on the ground.

"Yes, of course I will help her," she says kindly. "Now come on, you need to direct me to where she is, don't you?" She smiles while pulling out a wheelchair from a closet.

I smile to myself. Unfortunately, I completely forget about the loud noise until I open up the door. It is worse than before.

"Oh my goodness! What is that horrible sound?" the nurse shrieks.

"I have no clue, but let's go!"

We "run" across the hall, and I opened the door to stage D. I tell the nurse to wait at the back of the room and go up to the Teachers Only row and sit down. When I sit down, I tell my aunt that the nurse is waiting at the back of the room and that she should go and get her, so she does. My aunt waits in the back for about three minutes and then comes back with the nurse and the wheelchair.

"Ma'am, your sister here told me what was going on. Now, if you don't mind, I'm just going to wrap up your foot really, really quickly," says the nurse.

"How long will it take?"

"No more than twenty minutes."

"Okay."

"Alrighty then, why don't you just hop in the wheelchair."

My mom doesn't necessarily hop into the wheelchair. It is more of a slow process by which there is a lot of moaning, groaning, and grunting.

"All set?" asks the nurse.

"As ready as I'll ever be," replies my mom.

"Okay, then we had better be on our way!"

"See you," I say.

"Bye," she replies.

Then the crowd of people from wigs to suits swallows them whole.

Chapter 12

What Happened?

When my mom left, the whole row of Mullins went into quiet question mode. They couldn't really talk since they were right behind the judges, but they were dying to find out what was happening.

Madge can't help herself and whispers, "Where is she going?"

"What happened?" questions Lanie.

"Yeah, what did happen?" interrogates Alice while holding her arms up and looking totally confused.

"Ginny, seriously, what happened?" asks Daisy.

"Okay, okay, I'll tell you, but geez, guys, relax. So my mom and I were walking back from the bathroom this morning early and she tripped and fell over her high heels."

"So that's it? No FBI, Secret Service, CIA undercover? Not even a single cop? Well, that's a little boring," says Alice.

"Whoa, guys, hold your horses. First off, this is a dance competition, not a new episode of *Criminal Minds*. Second off, she's pregnant."

My aunt bends down and tells us to zip it and that we will have the conversation elsewhere. We look at each other and wisely keep our mouths shut!

"So, guys, who wants a smoothie because I'm going to go and get one!" I say.

"Count me in!" says Lanie.

"Me too!" says Madge.

"Me three," says Alice.

"Me four," says Daisy.

"Oh, all right, I'll come. Do you want me to pay?" asks my aunt.

"Sure, if you want," I say.

"Okay, let's go!" says Alice.

Chapter 13

What Happened, Part 2

We all order our Tropical Mix Smoothies (that is the store's name) and then sit down at a little table that is really beat down and crummy, but it is the nicest one there.

I get a banana, raspberry, and strawberry smoothie. It sounds weird, but it is actually really good!

"So do you guys want to go back?" I ask.

No one disagrees. This part of the convention center is kind of a pigpen!

"Guys, you wait here, I'm going to get a smoothie for Annabelle," says my aunt.

She comes back three minutes later with a banana, strawberry, and raspberry smoothie for my mom, and then we leave.

When we get back, we find my mom sitting right where we had left her a few minutes ago. The only thing that is different is the fact that now she has crutches and one of those cloth casts that you get in the emergency room before the specialist sees you and puts on the real plaster one.

My aunt hands her the smoothie and asks what they said.

"Well," my mom says, "we went into the hall area and there was this high-pitched sound that was extremely loud. I got such a shock that I almost passed out. Then we got into the little hospital room and the walls in there blocked off all the loud noise. The nurse sat me down and looked at my foot. I could hardly get my gym shoe off, it hurt so much, and I almost fainted the second time when I looked at my foot. It had gotten so much worse than before. She asked me if I could walk on it. I tried, but when I got off the chair and put pressure on it, it hurt so much! I have to admit that I actually couldn't even stand on it. Then they took an x-ray of my foot, and it turns out that that the roof of my foot is fractured."

"Oh no," I say.

"Wow, so two Mullins from the same family have broken feet, that's a real setback!" says Alice.

Lanie elbows Alice in her side.

"What the heck was that for?" says Alice.

"Don't rub it in!" says Lanie.

"So I guess that you won't be able to watch the U8s tomorrow then," says my aunt.

"Oh yes, I will!" my mom says with her mind set—family pride!

"Are you sure?"

"I'm positive!"

"Well, okay then," says my aunt uneasily.

"Oh, don't worry, I'll be fine!" says my mom.

But hearing this makes me wonder. I mean, like, she's pregnant! The baby has been in her for five months already. Did that what's-it chord strangle the baby when she fell? Babies are very delicate after all.

I get really close to my mom and whispers, "Mom, what is when you fell, what if the chord thingamabob choked the baby?"

"Oh, don't worry, that didn't happen," she says.

"Okay fine, but if it does, I'm warning you that I warned you!"

"Okay, now settle down and be quiet!" she says.

"Okay, geez!"

"Calling competitors 154 to 183 backstage, and please check in your number before you go backstage, thank you!" says the Witch.

Wait, the Witch isn't the announcer anymore. I wonder what trouble she is up to now! I'm deciding to leave her alone for once and stop sticking my nose up in other people's business even though she is pretty darn good at that too!

"Mom," I ask.

"Yes," she replies.

"Do you have any gum?"

"Sure, just let me get it out."

She reaches into her purse and pulls out a pack of gum that is still in the brand-new wrapper. Yet when I open it up, I find another surprise—there are dead bugs in every single one of the little pockets where the pieces of gum were supposed to be. Gross.

Delicious

Not so much

"Mom, I think that you should see this," I say, handing her the pack of gum.

I tell her to flip the pack over and look at it. The look on her face is a mixture of horror, surprise, and shock, and the noise that she makes is a cross between a gasp of horror and a gasp of surprise.

"What are those?" she whispers in disgust.

"Dead bugs and do you want to know what's funny?"

"What?" she asks.

"It's not even close to Halloween!"

"True," she agrees while still staring at the gum pack with *nothing* but surprise on her face!

"Mom, calm down, it's just a pack of dead bugs!" I say totally sarcastically!

"Daisy, why don't you go practice in the corner?" says my aunt Jackie.

"Fine," replies Daisy.

"Why don't you guys criticize her?" says my aunt.

"Works with me!" says Alice.

"Okay let's go!" says Madge.

When we leave, Lanie whispers to me, "I wonder what they are talking about since they want so much privacy!"

"I have absolutely no clue!"

"Okay."

"I really love your dress," I say. It is blue and all sparkles with plain white silk connecting two buckles. It has puffy sleeves and white lace down her arms with blue sequins sewn into it. There is a sparkly, puffy skirt with lace lining it, and the cape is a little white bow. It might be my favorite one that my aunt ever designed!

"Have you seen Maggie's dress?" she asks.

"No, what does it look like?"

It's white with pale pink flowers and a hot pink design going down around her. There are pink butterflies going up the sleeves and a pink design going up around them. The skirt is a pale pink and hot pink and has white ruffles, and the cape is a pink and white butterfly.

"Wow, that sounds really pretty for her!"

"Yeah, it is," she says but is really sidetracked.

"So how's Charlotte?" I ask.

"She's okay."

Lanie's younger sister Charlotte was in a car crash when she was younger. Her leg never fully healed like the doctors thought it would, and she hasn't been able to walk on it since. It has been getting worse and worse and that is not a good sign. She's the one that I used to cover for Paige when she called me Gin. However, Lanie's sister's name is *not* Alex.

"Okay, what's wrong?"

"She's not good at all," she replies with her voice cracking.

"How?" I ask.

"She went to the doctor a last week because her leg was hurting super bad. The doctor said that if she couldn't move it in forty-eight hours, then she would have to get surgery to remove it! And guess what?" she says.

"What?"

"She couldn't move it at all!"

"Oh my gosh, I'm so sorry! When's the surgery?" I ask her with sorrow.

"Tomorrow at two, but she's staying at the hospital until then," she replies while starting to cry.

"Lanie, shhhh. You'll ruin your makeup," I say trying to calm her down. "Hey, do you want to sleep in my room tonight?"

"Sure, I'll ask my mom when we go back."

I feel horrible for her. I mean, I always have known that this will eventually come but not now, not now with nationals right here.

The doctors said that one day it would get so bad that she would have to "heal" it. In a way, it is better because now she can get a prosthetic and *finally* be able to walk again for the first time in over five years. She is ten, so the accident happened when she was five. Oh well, for Charlottes' birthday, I will get her something really good (her birthday is December 10).

Chapter 14

Daisy Dances

Key Items
1. 📱 phone
2. 🗺 map
3. 👛 wallet
4. ✏ concealer
5. ✏ sharpies

Right when we get back from reviewing Daisy's steps, the lady next to the stage says, "Calling competitors numbers 181 to 102 backstage please, and before you go backstage, please check in your number. Thank you."

"Good luck, Daisy, you'll do *great*!" I say.

"Thanks!"

Everyone else chips in saying exactly what I said . . . again.

"Lanie, are you going to ask your Mom about sleeping over tonight?" I whisper to her.

"Yeah, right now."

"Hey, Mom, may Lanie sleep over in our room tonight?"

"I don't know, Ginny, just remember that we are not leaving tomorrow like everybody else."

"Oh right." I turned to Lanie and say, "Lanie, just so you know, we're not leaving tomorrow like you guys are."

"Yeah, I know I already worked that out. We are meeting my mom at 8:00 a.m. in the lobby and will leave then, so I will have to get up latest at 7:30. Will you be up by then?"

"Yep, no problem, we will make sure you are at the lobby at 8:00 a.m.!"

"Cool, then it is okay with my mom."

"Mom."

"Mm, mm?" she replies while looking at a stage handbook.

"Lanie is sleeping in our room. Her mom said okay as long as we can have her in the lobby latest at 8:00 a.m."

"Great," she says sarcastically.

"Do you have any water?" I ask her while praying that it isn't poisoned.

"Here," my mom handed me a bottle without looking at it.

"Mom, this is spoiled milk!" I say while looking into the bottle and scrunching up my nose.

"What! Let me see."

I look up at the lady next to the stage and see that it is the Witch and that she is grinning her snake-like smile at me while chuckling to herself. I knew that she was behind all this—the skunk M&M's, the rotten milk, the poisoned water, the bug gum. I just wish I can somehow prove it, but most of all I wish she will just stop it all so I didn't have to worry so much.

"Guys, look, it's Daisy!" says Lanie.

Daisy has a *brand-new* dress that literally arrived this morning. Thank goodness it fits! It is turquoise with sewn-in scales. It almost looks like a mermaid. In fact the back piece is a mermaid's tail. The skirt has white ruffles with blue sparkles.

Hornpipe is her best dance. She just can't blow it I think to myself.

"There she goes!" says Aunt Annabelle.

Bang, and a rally knock toe bang toe, and a rally bang rally step high click and toe switch. Click click and toe hop spin bang toe and rally hop back tip and knock and bang toe. Left toe toe toe tip and bang twirl and rally bang rally knock and a heel, heel toe and rally hop back brush brush and toe bang rally toe rally hop back.

"That was awesome!" says Lanie to Daisy as she walks off stage.

"Thanks," says Daisy while gasping for air (if you haven't noticed already, Irish dancing is really hard work!).

Chapter 15

Recalls

Now, instead of telling the whole story of the soft shoe round or just skipping the whole thing, I decide to sum it all up.

How Daisy, Lanie, Madge, and Alice Did

Daisy—Her strong side is hard shoe. She did great in her soft shoes too. (It will even out to amazing!)

Lanie—She is amazing because soft shoes is her strong side. (She is awesome well in her hard shoes, so again it will all even out to great!)

Madge—She did great besides the fact that she tripped a little bit. (That doesn't take off points though—thank goodness!) In her hard-shoe round, she did good though!

Alice—She did amazing! (Alice is just the opposite of Daisy—her soft shoes are her strong side, and her hard shoes could be better.)

Anyway, I just want to get to recalls (recalls are where you see if you qualified to do your set dance—or not.)

-♪♪♪-

"Ladies and gentlemen, I have the recalls for competition 2 under twelve girls," says the Witch.

As soon as she starts talking, the whole hall goes quiet as church mice. (Just so you know, the first recall number is always 101).

"Number 101.

"Number 102. ['*Yes!*' I say while shaking Daisy.]

"Number 103.

"Number 105.

"Number 106. ['Yes! Great job, Lanie,' says my aunt.]

"Number 108.

"Number 109.

"Number 111.

"Number 112.

"Number 115.

"Number 116.

"Number 118.

"Number 119.

"Number 120.

"Number 124.

"Number 127.

"Number 128.

"Number 130.

"Number 130.

"Number 137. ['What, *no*! That can't be,' whispers Madge, starting to cry.]

"Number 138

"Number 139 ['Yes! Congratulations, Alice.']

"Number 147.

"Number 149.

"Number 150.

"Number 151.

"Number 154.

"Number 156.

"Number 160.

"Number 161.

"Number 162.

"Number 163.

"Number 167.

"Number 170.

"Number 176.

"Number 182.

"Number 183.

"Number 184.

"Number 189.

"Number 191.

"Number 195.

"Number 200.

"Number 201.

"Number 202.

"Number 207.

"Number 209.

"Number 210.

"Number 211.

"Number 212.

"Number 213.

"Number 214.

"Number 216.

"Number 218.

"Number 219.

"Number 221.

"Number 222.

"Number 224.

"Number 226.

"Number 227.

"Number 229.

"And number 230.

"Thank you, and if your number was called, please come to the front and check in your number please."

I always hate leaving the room after recalls. There are cheers and cries; it's simply *not* a good mix.

I feel really bad for Madge. I know that tripping doesn't take any points off, but I think that nerves got the best of her, and she just wasn't able to dance her best.

I go to give her a hug and tell her that she did great anyway, but she won't let me. I guess she just wants to be left alone for a while. Because whatever we say to her wouldn't change the fact that she just didn't dance well enough for a recall.

Great. Now I will have to get *two* great birthday gifts! (Madge's is August 29.)

Chapter 16

Calie McDaniel

"Shake it off! You will get them next year!" says my aunt to Madge.

"How about a nice lunch to get our minds off of dancing?" says my mom.

"Fine," says Madge.

As we are walking, I see a little girl who looks scared, lost, and alone. At first I don't recognize her, but then it hits me—she is Caroline McDaniel's little sister, Calie. They look alike, but Calie doesn't have a wig and makeup on!

I point her out to my mom and say, "Mom, that is Caroline McDaniel's little sister."

"Oh yeah, what's her name again?" she asks.

"Calie, and, Mom, she looks lost."

"A little bit, but, honey, we can't just walk up and go. Hi, Calie, we're going to go and take you to your mommy."

"Why not?" I ask.

"Because we don't know the family, and we don't know where the mom is or what she looks like."

"Well, obviously she is going to be by Caroline, watching her practice."

"Ginny, look at me." I look at her. "We don't know them and no matter what you say, the answer will still be a no."

A few seconds ago, I notice Calie get up and start walking toward my mom and me. I don't say anything because I don't really want to get blamed—as I usually do! Also, because she will make a "what the heck" face at me and make me feel all guilty. She will also think that I had called her over, which I didn't do.

"Um, ethcuthe me," says Calie while pulling on my mom's sweater (it is cold in the convention center).

Now that I get a good look at her, I can tell that she has been crying. Her eyes and her nose are red and she keeps on sniffling.

"I can't find my mommy and I am lotht," she says.

"Don't worry, we will help you find her," says my mom to Calie then looking to me like "What did I tell you!"

"I recognithed you from the dantherth handbook as a danth teacher tho I thaw you and athked you for help!"

"Well, I am glad that you chose me to help you," says my mom.

"Who are you?" she asks me while completely ignoring my mom.

"I'm Ginny. I'm her daughter."

"Why is your thtomach tho big?" she asks my mom.

My mom's face starts to burn, but she quickly forces herself to calm down and answers, "Because I'm expecting."

"What, a new toy? Can I have it!" asks Calie, getting super excited!

"No, a baby," says my mom getting ready to burst.

"Oh! Ith it a boy or a girl?"

"We don't know yet."

"Why?"

"Because we want it to be a surprise." She turns and looks at me. "Ginny, I am going to go and tell the others that we are going to be a little late for lunch."

Obviously she doesn't want to be with Calie for one more second (and hey, I can't blame her!).

"Wait here and *don't* move," she says very strictly.

These are the times that I actually don't think of disobeying my mom, or else there will literally be lava exploding out to her head!

"What happened to your leg?" asks Calie.

"I broke it."

"How?"

"I was dancing."

"Oh. What happened to your mom's leg?"

"She fractured it."

"How?"

"She tripped and fell."

"Oh. Ith your mom really having a baby or ith tee jutht fat?" (she pronounces "she" as "tee").

"She's having a baby!" I snap, starting to get really irritated! No wonder my mom ditched us.

I notice her get up and start to walk away.

"Wait, where are you going?" I ask while trying to catch up with her.

"To find my mom."

"We have to wait here for my mom."

"Why?"

"Because she told us to."

I am starting to realize what a piece of work she is.

"I'm leaving."

"Come here!" I say sternly through clenched teeth.

"Why?"

"So . . . um . . . you could . . . um, tell me about your sister," I quickly answer.

"Okay!"

"Well then, tell me about her! Is she nice, mean, funny? Tell me!"

"Well, thometimth tee ith nithe and thometimth tee ith mean."

"Oh, goodie, here's my mom." Thank goodness!

"Hi!" says Calie.

"I have a game that we can play."

"Yeah! I love gameth!"

"This game is called the silent game."

"How do you play?"

"Well, you have to stay quiet to win this game and whoever stays quiet the longest wins a piece of candy."

"Okay."

"When I say quiet, you have to be quiet."

"Okay."

"Quiet."

Man, it is a relief to have her stop talking. She reminds me of a broken record. Going on and on!

My mom makes the time-out signal and then Calie starts yapping again.

"Why did you make that thignal? Doeth it mean that we can thalk again?"

"Well obviously," I whisper to myself.

"Okay, I just realized we can't find your mom without you, so you can talk but not that much."

"Okay."

"So what does your mom look like?"

"She hath thort brown hair and blue eyeth, and oh goodie, there tee ith!"

She runs over to her mom and gives her a big hug, and her mom thanks us.

"Bye, Calie," I say.

"By, Ginny and Mrth. Mullinth!"

"Bye," says my mom.

"Man, she's a piece of work!"

"Yeah, let's hurry, otherwise we won't be able to eat lunch."

"Okay."

Chapter 17

Set Dances

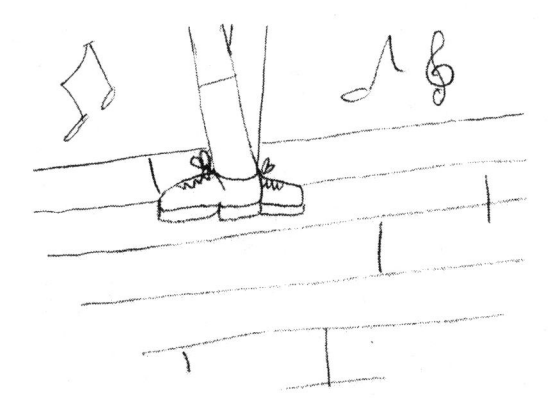

"Sorry we're late, but we just had to save a lost girl who sure was a handful," I say.

"You don't have your food yet? You didn't have to wait for us," says my mom.

"Oh, we didn't. Our food is on the way," says Alice.

Madge elbows her in the ribs.

"What was that for?"

"Just shut up!"

"Guys stop, here's the waiter with our food," says my aunt.

"Hello, would you like something to drink, or for that matter, something to eat?"

"Sure, I will have a Diet Coke and cheese pizza," I reply to the waitress.

"I'll have a Diet Coke and a Caesar salad," says my mom.

"Okay, I'll be right back."

A few minutes later, the waiter comes back with our food and drinks. You can tell how bummed Madge is, she is really trying to hold back her tears, and she has hardly touched her food but only picked at it. I don't know what I would've done if I didn't get recalled. You work so hard for it for months just for it to be thrown away. You get a pretty dress, your teachers say that you look wonderful, but then you find out that you weren't good enough. I think I just would have wanted to go home and sulk, but poor Madge has to stay and eat with us all before she leaves and put up a poker face. You can tell it is hard for her, but she doesn't want to destroy the joy for the girls who did recall and are super excited to dance.

"Eat quick, girls, you dance in half an hour!" my mom says.

Normally we go straight to dance our sets after recalls, but they announced there is going to be a delay with the judges being held up at another stage, so we have just enough time to eat, which is fine with me because I'm starving!

When we are all finished, we rush over to the stages for a quick practice in the hallway and to reapply more makeup to the overly decorated faces—more lipstick and lip liner is definitely needed after eating!

Alice's set dance is called the Drunken Gauger, Lanie's set dance is called the Kilkenny Races, and Daisy's set dance is called the Ace and Deuce of Pipering.

How Lanie, Alice, and Daisy did in their Set Dances . . .

Alice—She did great on her set; she could've been higher up on her toes though.

Lanie—She did well. Her steps sounded a little muffled though. I couldn't really make it out even though I memorized them. She scored high on her other steps, and she will get a very good score!

Daisy—*Daisy did her set dance absolutely perfectly!* I would be so jealous if I were dancing! (She didn't fall, just in case you were wondering—I get fifty dollars! *Yeah!*)

Chapter 18

Patrick

After everyone does their sets, we have a full hour before we had to be at awards. Awards is where you find out how well you placed based on the three dances that you performed. I'm not hungry since we just ate lunch. I am thirsty though.

"Mom, I am going to go and get a sip of water," I say while getting up from my seat.

"Hold up, we've got some right here," she says while reaching into her purse.

"No offense or anything, but I don't really trust asking you for water from *our* bottles anymore."

I go out into the hallway and take a sip of water from the nearest water fountain.

When I get up from the water fountain, I turn around and bump into somebody. I look up and try not to blush while time stops around me!

He is cute—*really* cute!

"Oh, I'm so sorry!" I say.

"No, no, no, don't be," he says.

His voice is as smooth as a summer ocean breeze.

"Hi, I'm Ginny," I say to him hoping that he doesn't automatically think of Harry Potter!

"I'm Patrick."

He has curly red hair and a bunch of freckles.

"How did you hurt your foot?" he asks.

"Oh, I broke it dancing," I say, looking down at my orange cast.

"That stinks."

"So," I say, trying to change the subject, "why are you here? Do you dance?"

"No, my sister does. She's nine."

"Oh, I would be dancing, but, you know."

"Yeah, how old are you?"

"I'm twelve, you?"

"Thirteen."

"Listen, I have to get back to my stage, you can come if you want," I say, praying to the Man Upstairs that he will say sure!

"Okay, what stage are you on?" he asks.

"Um, I am on D."

"Cool, I am on C, so I'll meet you by the entrance."

I wait at the entrance for about three minutes, and then Patrick comes walking out of the stage C room.

"Hey, instead do you want to go and get a smoothie?" he asks me.

"Sure."

"What dance school are you with?" he asks me.

"I am at Mullins School of Irish Dance, my mom's the owner."

"That's cool, my sister is at O'Keefe."

"Cool, do you have any other siblings?" I ask him.

"Well, I have a baby brother, Matthew, a younger sister, Mallory, who is dancing, and an older sister. Do you? I mean have any sisters or brothers?"

"I have a younger brother named Charlie, a little sister named Bella, and my mom is pregnant."

"That's cool, boy or girl?"

"I don't know," I say just as we got to the smoothie stand.

Patrick chooses a strawberry, banana, blueberry, and raspberry smoothie, and I choose the same.

I text my mom while we are waiting for the smoothies.

Mom I'm at the smoothie stand. I met someone adorable! I'll b back in 45 min. b back before awards.

K have fun, love you.

"So," I say as we get our smoothies, "when's your birthday?"

"July 3, how about you?"

"August 13."

"The smoothies here are really good."

"Yeah, I had one earlier," I say awkwardly.

"So what's your middle name?" he asks.

"Rose, you?

"Andrew."

"Do you want to come over to where we are sitting for awards?" I ask him.

I can't believe I just asked him that. I'm sure he has plenty of friends he would rather sit with besides my group of friends and me. I feel my cheeks turning red from embarrassment, but to my surprise, he says he would like to! I mean *unreal*, right?

"I'll need to tell my mom though. Otherwise she will totally flip out."

"Yeah, mine too."

"Do you have a phone?" he asks. "Of course you do, you were just texting your mom when we ordered the smoothies. . . . Sorry," he says while rubbing his gorgeous red hair.

Okay I really need to focus on the conversation, but it is just so hard when a totally cute boy is talking to you and I am just about to have a heart attack from nervousness!

"I can give you my number," he says, smiling at me.

"Okay," I say while this time I am sure my heart stopped.

I look up at his blue eyes, and they are smiling at me and I smile back. Just so I am not too obvious, I quickly get my phone out but drop it. Gosh, I am so clumsy. We both bent down to get it and our hands touched. His hands feel warm and I am sure my hands are all sweaty! He hands the phone to me and we exchange numbers. I really hope I take the right number down because I am not sure I completely trust myself right now! We go into the awards auditorium and find some seats.

Chapter 19

Awards

"Ginny, where were you?" asks Daisy.

She does a double take on Patrick, not really sure if he is with me or not (lucky me, he is). She looks dumbstruck when she realized he is with me! I know, right?! I try to sound really cool.

"Daisy that's Patrick. Patrick that's Daisy."

"Hey," says Patrick.

"Oh cool, eh, I mean hi."

Daisy sits down with us, and I see Alice and Lanie look over and Alice winks.

"Ladies and gentlemen, I have the results for today's competitions."

Everyone cheers and then the room becomes silent.

"First, I am going to be announcing the U8 Ceili mixed."

It goes on like that until the lady finally gets to the U12 girls solo dances.

"Now we have the U12 girls solo dancing awards. Would all of you girls please make your way backstage."

Daisy, Alice, and Lanie leave for the stage.

"Congrats on your sister getting fifth," I say to Patrick.

"Yeah, I hope that all your friends do good too," he says to me.

"Thanks, I'm sure that they will," I say, looking away.

"First, I am going to call up the top ten . . . Daisy Mullins O' Connley number 102,"

"Okay, good," I say.

"Margret Vincenelli number 187, Alice Green number 139."

"Yes!"

"Kory Lee number 198, Molly Jackson number 188, Ally Taylor number 208, Bridget Cox number 125, Sarah Butler number 132, and Lanie Sullivan number 106."

"Yes! Okay, so all three of them are in the top ten."

Alice, Lanie, Daisy, and all the other girls who place in the top ten go and stand behind the podium.

I'm skipping to the top fifteen because all the Mullins dancers place in the top ten.

"15, Caroline McDaniel number 127—"

"She got fifteenth? Wow!"

"—14, Ella Ericson number 272,

"13, Mary Adams number 103,

"12, Cece Turner number 207,

"11, Catherine Brooks number 173,

"10, Margaret Vincenelli number 187,

"9, Bridget Cox number 125,

"8, Molly Jackson number 188,

"7, Sarah Butler number 132,

"6, Ally Taylor number 208,

"5, Lanie Sullivan number 106—"

"Yeah! Way to go Lanie!" I scream.

"—4, Kory Lee number 198,

"3, Kelly Duncan number 146,

"2, Alice Green number 139."

"Woohoo! Yeah, Alice!" I yell.

"And the winner for the 2015 American Nationals is number 102, Daisy Mullins O'Connley of Mullins School of Irish Dance!" says the announcer.

"Woohoo! Yeah, go Daisy!" I am screaming so loud, my ears are ringing! I crutch up to the stage to get a better view. "Yeah, Daisy! Good job!"

My mom and my aunt go up to the stage to take a picture as the dance teachers.

They put a sash around her, gave her a little tiara, a silver platter with the words "1st Place Nationals" engraved on it, and an absolutely *huge* trophy!

She is smiling like there is no tomorrow, and frankly, I can't really blame her! Patrick smiles at me and says, "That's your cousin right?"

I nod, smile back, and say, "Yeah."

"You two sort of look alike," he says basically to himself.

The U12 competition takes a final bow—twice—and then finally heads off to the stage.

I crutch toward Daisy, Alice, and Lanie as fast as I can and then hug them all! We are all laughing, hugging, and smiling like nothing could ever go wrong!

My mom and my Aunt Jackie hug Daisy, Lanie, and Alice really hard.

"I knew that you guys could do it!" I say to all of them.

"I don't know what to say! I am so happy!" exclaims Daisy.

"Me too!" says Alice.

"Me three," says Lanie.

Daisy, Alice, Lanie, and I all went and sat down back where Patrick and I were sitting before.

"You guys really did amazing!" I say to all of them.

"Yeah, good job!" says Patrick.

-♪♪♪-

When we get back from awards, everyone is beat! Lanie goes and grabs her bag for our "sleepover." When she gets back, we change into our pj's and get ready for bed, but we don't go to bed just quite yet.

"So who is that guy that you were sitting with?" asks Lanie.

"His name is Patrick. I ran into him when I went to go and get a drink of water," I say. No need to specify anything.

"He's kind of cute."

"Yeah, I guess," I say while trying really hard to not look *that* interested!

"Why did he leave right after we basically sat down?"

"I have actually no clue. . . . He was looking a little fidgety though."

Come to wonder, why did he leave right after he said "good job"? His mom must have texted him when I went up to congratulate Lanie, Alice, and Daisy. Yeah, that must be it.

"Yeah, anyway, you did *amazing* today!"

I can't help but remember the reason that I invited her over here today. Her sister. I feel absolutely horrible!

I guess it must have shown because all of a sudden she says, "Ginny, I know what you are thinking about, but personally, I would really appreciate it if we don't talk about it."

"Okay, perfect."

"So what—"

I cut her off before she could finish,

"You are so lucky that you don't have to be here tomorrow!" I blurt out. I don't even know where that came from!

"No, Ginny, you are lucky that you don't have to be where I have to be tomorrow."

And guess what, she's right. I am lucky to have a little brother and a little sister who are healthy, a foot that will actually heal in a few months, not never! Lanie's family is the one that needs some luck.

"Anyway—" I say, but before I could finish, my mom cuts me off. Man, cutting people off must run in the family.

"Ginny and Lanie, time to go to sleep, we all have a big day tomorrow."

"Okay," says Lanie.

"Fine," I say, grouchier, but as soon as the lights are out, I instantly fall asleep.

Chapter 20

U8 Solo's Wake-Up Call

"Ginny, Ginny, *Ginny, wake up!*"

My mom is standing on top of me and nearly screams my head off. Geez, zero patience. Her face is green and all puffed up, and her hair is a mess! Wow! Pregnancy sure does make you miserable.

"What time is it?" I ask her.

"Six, get Lanie up too!" she says impatiently.

Lanie looks like a baby when she sleeps, like no harm in the world would ever come to her ever! It is almost a shame to wake her up, but I have to.

"Lanie, Lanie, Lanie, get up!" I say, shaking her gently like a little rag doll.

"What!" she screams at me. Well, like mother, like daughter!

"Sorry," I say, laughing.

"Why did you wake me up?"

"Because we have to get ready."

"What time is it?" she says, stretching and rubbing her eyes so much I am afraid they will fall out.

"Six," I say, "now come on."

She gets up and stretches out her arms and cracks her back. Ugh, I hate when people do that!

While I get ready in the bathroom and do my hair (I have a braid in again), someone knocks on the door; it is room service. One more thing crossed off my bucket list.

"Thank you," says my mom to the person who delivered the food.

I have an omelet and hash browns. They are delicious!

-♪♪♪-

Right after we finish, we head out to the lobby where we are supposed meet Lanie's mom. When we see her, we say our good-byes, good-lucks, and thank-yous to each other. Then we hurry downstairs.

We get to the practice room, and as usual, Aunt Jackie is already there.

Today is the U8 girls' solos. Paige and Maggie and all the others are already there too. Daisy is sitting on a chair next to her mom. Today she isn't tired at all! She is wearing her first-place sash and bouncing up and down with excitement!

"So I can tell you are excited, and I'll take that fifty dollars off your hands whenever you're ready."

"Tomorrow, okay?"

"Fine, I'm going to go and get a smoothie, do you want to come?"

"Sure."

"Mom, we'll be back in twenty minutes."

"Okay, no more than twenty minutes, we are starting soon."

"Okay," I reply.

We get out of the practice room and walk straight to the Tropical Mix smoothie stand. I order a strawberry, banana, raspberry, and blueberry smoothie. I know, but I just have to order the same one as I had with Patrick yesterday; so it reminds me of him. Daisy orders a blackberry and strawberry smoothie. We find a wall bench and sit down.

All of a sudden, I hear my phone make the tweety bird sound, which means I got a text. The text is from Patrick! I almost jump out of my seat, but instead I elbow Daisy really hard.

"What the heck?" she snaps at me.

"Patrick texted me!"

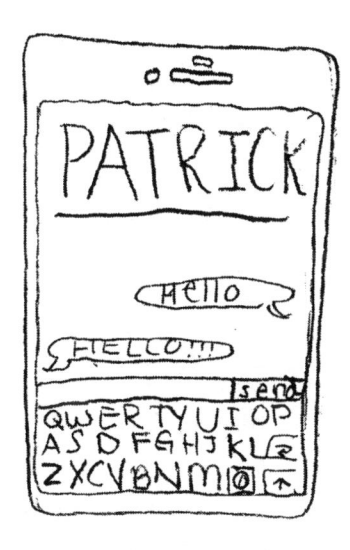

"Really? What did he say?" she asks, totally changing reactions.

"Hi, r u going to b here today??? I no that u r busy w/ your mom being a dance teacher..."

I reply, "Yeah, we r goin to b here but I have to watch my cousins and help drill, u can come if u want."

"Wait, is Patrick's last name Fisher?" Daisy asks me.

"I don't know."

"Because there is a boy who lives a few houses down from me and he has curly red hair too. He goes to the public school, but the Patrick Fisher who lives close to me is transferring to our school.

"Um... I'm not sure... here, let me ask him."

I get out my phone and text him. "By the way, is your last name Fisher???"

He replies right away. "Yeah, how did u know???"

"Daisy! His last name is Fisher!"

"Awesome!" she says.

"Well my cousin Daisy lives on 351 Oakly Drive and right down the street is a person with the last name Fisher and his name is Patrick . . . Do you live on Oakly Drive???"

"Yeah."

"Daisy! He does!"

"Awesome! I knew it! See how you always need me. Without you still would have thought that he is a stranger." She keeps on rambling on and on and on.

"Do u want to meet at stage B . . . That's where my cousins r dancing and we can watch them together if u want . . ." I text him.

"My mom said yes . . . C ya in about 10 min."

"Bye!" I say.

"Bye," he replies.

"Well, Daisy, while you were talking to yourself about how *great* you are, I got Patrick to come sit with us at the stage," I say really smugly, trying really hard to hide my sheer excitement!

"Really? Cool!"

"Yeah, I know," I say. It is weird though. Now matter how good I feel in this hotel, I always feel like there is someone or something constantly watching me, but every time I turn around, there is nothing there. Odd.

When Daisy and I finish our smoothies, we head toward stage B. Right when we get there, Patrick shows up. He has a Blackhawks sweatshirt on, basketball shoes, and baggy shorts. Also, his irresistible curly red hair was all over the place—*adorable!*

"Hi," I say. Come on, Ginny, can't you think of anything better to say!

"Hey," he says.

"You remember Daisy, right?" I say to him, feeling like a completely idiot.

"Yeah, um . . . hi," he says to Daisy.

"Hi," she says to him while looking back down at her gym shoes.

"Do you guys want to go and find a spot by the stage?" I ask.

"Sure," Patrick says.

We head in there, and five times I almost trip over people's feet with my crutches. I hate these stupid things! We find an open spot on the floor and sit down.

"Ladies and gentlemen, it is time to start the U8 girls' solo dancing competition," says the announcer next to the stage. "Will all the dancers please come to check in there number here please?" says the lady with a very Southern accent.

"Oh great, not her again!" I say without thinking.

"Who?" asks Daisy and Patrick.

"Oh, sorry, the announcer next to the stage," I say trying not to emphasize too much.

"What did she ever do," he asks while looking up to the lady, "Oh, wait! I know her!"

"You do?" I ask him harshly. "How?"

"Well, she is a mom at our dance school. Her daughter is a U8 and . . . yep, that's all I've got," he says.

"What *did* she ever do to you?" asks Daisy to me.

"Don't think I'm crazy, but she put rotten milk in my water bottle and tried to poison my water. You remember the skunk M&M's, Daisy? Not to mention, *broke into my hotel room and tried to steal a bunch of stuff*, and put dead bugs in my gum pack, and I am sure that she will do more!"

"That does sound like her actually," says Patrick.

"How?" I demand.

"Well, my mom doesn't like her because she is obsessed with her daughter winning and is always bugging the teachers to move her daughter up even though she shouldn't be."

"Yeah, what else?" I ask.

"My mom is always saying how annoying and pushy and bossy she is. To sum it up, the lady is basically just obsessed with her daughter winning, and I've heard that her daughter actually doesn't want to dance anymore because of her mom."

"I don't know about you guys, but I think that we should find out more," says Daisy.

"I'm in!" I say.

"Why not!" says Patrick.

"Hold on, guys, listen," I say to them.

"Could you take over for a minute? I have to go and talk to my daughter about something very important," says the Witch to the other lady next to the stage.

"Yeah, okay, ten minutes at the most though," says the other lady to the Witch.

"Fine," retorts the Witch.

The Witch leaves, and I say to Daisy and Patrick, "I think that we should start investigating now."

Chapter 21

Proof

I've read enough spy books to know how to spy on people. After all, how do you think I know that we are getting another puppy this Christmas. (It is a shih tzu, and it is already trained.) Like I said, I'm pretty good!

The three of us get up without a plan trying to look all normal as if we are just going for another smoothie; however, Daisy really sucks. She's trying too hard to look like a detective and looks left and right too see if anyone is noticing us.

"The coast is clear," she says loudly.

Patrick and I look at each other and he raises his eyebrows. We smile at each other, and I can hardly hold in my laugh. I am seriously considering if it wouldn't be better to leave Daisy behind because if we are going to be successful following the Witch, she better shape up or ship out. But then I look at her excited face and sparkly eyes, and I know there is no way I can let her miss out. Well, hopefully we won't get caught!

We stand against the wall while the Witch goes backstage to where all the dancers are.

When she comes out with what must be her daughter, I say to Daisy and Patrick, "Hey, do you guys want to go and get some smoothies?" loud enough so that the Witch can hear me but not suspect anything.

I wink at them and Daisy winks back at me three times and *so extremely* obviously. Why doesn't she just let the whole world know that we are going to spy on the Witch? After I settle down my really short temper, we follow her out.

The hallway still doesn't have the really loud shrieking noise, and I am overjoyed about that.

We follow the Witch until she makes a turn into the Staff Only room.

"Okay, I'll wait here and you guys go and get a smoothie," I say loudly again.

"Okay, let's go," Patrick says to Daisy, who winks obviously again.

Oh my gosh, is she bad at this.

As soon as they start walking away, I press my ear against the door. Luckily it isn't another soundproof room! I pull out my phone and go under Voice Memos and start to record their conversation just as the Witch starts to speak. "Ava, I swear I've done everything that I can in my power to make you win. I've put sour milk in their water, I broke into their room, *I even broke her mom's foot!*" she says as I gasp and try to hold myself back.

"Okay, but, Mom, if I don't win, I really don't want to dance anymore," says Ava to the Witch.

"But if you do win, which I think that you will, you will keep on dancing until you make it to Worlds." (You can only qualify for Worlds if you are a U10.)

"Mom, no!"

"Oh yes!"

I listen in shock. What type of parent forces their child to do something that they obviously don't like? Although I don't understand how anyone could not like dancing!

"Now, let's go and win this thing!"

As soon as I start to hear the Witch say this, I stop the recording and quickly hide behind the nearest pillar, which luckily isn't that far away. They head in the opposite direction, and I hurry toward the smoothie stand where Daisy and Patrick are sitting at a bench.

As soon as they see me, they jump to their feet and hurry toward me without drawing attention to themselves. Daisy is awful at this too!

"Go back to the bench," I say to them as we all strut to the bench where Daisy and Patrick were sitting a minute ago.

I pull out my phone again and start to play the recording.

"Ava, I swear I've done everything that I can in my power to make you win. I've put sour milk in their water, I broke into their room, *I even broke her mom's foot!*"

"Okay, but, Mom, if I don't win, I really don't want to dance anymore."

"But if you do win, which I think that you will, you will keep on dancing until you make it to Worlds."

"Mom, no!"

"Oh yes! Now, let's go and win this thing!'"

Daisy listens with her mouth open, and Patrick just stares at me like I just dropped from the sky and landed right in front of him.

"So all that nonsense that you were saying was true?" asks Daisy.

"What, so you didn't believe me?" I ask her.

"Well, I didn't actually think . . . that, um . . . you know . . . that someone would actually . . . um . . . do something like that except for in your head," she fumbles out quickly.

I just stare at her.

"You do kind of have a wild imagination sometimes."

I am absolutely stunned! She didn't believe me?

"Why did you act like such a spy then if you thought that it was all fake?" I ask her.

"Because I thought that it would be fun to do something that we used to do when we were younger."

"Guys, come on!" Patrick says. "Geez, Dad was right, women can be so complicated sometimes," he mumbles under his breath.

"Um, excuse me?" I ask him.

"Oh, nothing, nothing."

"Okay, so are you guys going to do it or what?" I ask them.

"Yep!" says Patrick.

"Okay," says Daisy still half-glaring at me. I do the same thing back. Oh my gosh. Patrick was right; women can be complicated!

I grab my phone and text my mom.

"I forgot something in the room, me daisy & Patrick r going to go & get it,"

"Ok do u have a key?"

"Yea," I reply.

"Ok . . . b back soon!"

"Bye."

"Guys, come on, we have to talk in private," I say to them.

Chapter 22

Game Plan

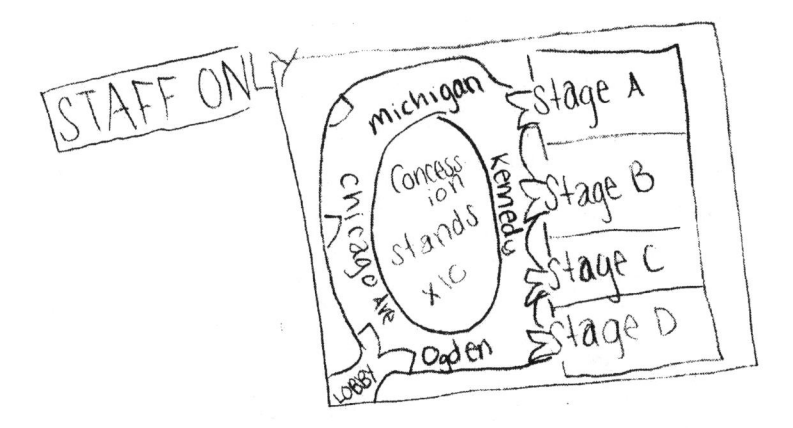

I turn and then we hurry toward the hotel part of the maze-sort-of place. Nationals are in a huge convention center that is connected to a hotel by a skywalk. It would be really cool if I wasn't afraid of heights.

We finally make to the door that leads to the skywalk. Dang! I forgot that there are like thirty thousand flights of stairs before we even make it to the skywalk.

"Guys, um, do you want to go and look for an elevator or something because I think that I might die if I have to go up all those stairs."

Daisy looks at my cast and nods. "Yeah, it probably would be best. . . . Plus, I don't feel like walking up that many stairs," she says while looking up.

"Yeah, me neither," says Patrick.

"Okay, let's go find one then," I say.

We walk out and ask the nearest person where the nearest elevator is.

"It should be right around the corner and then on your left," he says pointing.

"Okay, thanks!"

"Don't mention it," he says.

We head off in the direction that he told us, and I get a little bit nervous. What if he was working for the Witch? That means that we would be in trouble. However, I think that she works solo like the girl Foxface in the book *The Hunger Games*. We start walking (or in my case, crutching) in the direction that the man told us to go in to find the elevator, and surprisingly enough, the elevator is right in front of our eyes. We walk in, and I press the button for the skywalk. We cross the skywalk, and when we enter the hotel, we head straight for that floor's elevator. We get in and I press button 14 for our floor. When the elevator finally reaches our floor, we step out and turn left to our room. Our room number is 1411. Daisy's is 1413. I slide the key in, a little green light flashes, and I let us in.

"What are we going to do about the lady? Or whatever you call her, Ginny?" Daisy says.

"The Witch," I correct her. "And I'm not sure. Patrick, do you have any suggestions?"

"I do if you have a paper and some markers."

"Lucky you, I had to do something for sixteen hours in a car," I say.

I hurry over to my duffle and grab out the pad of paper and colored pencils that I brought. I pull them out with some difficulty and hand them to Patrick.

"You guys are so lucky that my sister made me walk around, get lost, and memorize every corner of that convention center maze! Just so that I could see all the bows and makeup!" he says, mocking.

I find it offensive. I don't like any of it, but it is a necessity to my *life!*

He draws a messy square on one of the sheets of paper and some doors, the skywalk, and then another square, which must be the hotel. That is where we are now.

"You guys are also lucky that I know that the Witch leaves the check-in counter at nine to announce the competition."

I look at my phone and check the time.

"Okay, we have an hour and forty-five minutes until nine," I say with confidence. We can come up with plan before then.

"Okay, so what are we going to do?" Daisy asks.

"I'll show you," Patrick says but does nothing.

"Well, show us," I say expectantly.

"Oh yeah!" he says, slapping his head.

Daisy rolls her eyes and I start to laugh.

"Well, she leaves the front desk at nine, so we have an hour and forty-five minutes until then."

"Yeah, we know that," Daisy says, getting irritated.

It really is pretty funny to just watch her.

"Next though, actually instead of going to announce the competition like she is supposed to, she actually goes to the ladies' room. I think it is to put on *more* makeup, but I don't know, I could be wrong."

"You most likely are," Daisy says under her breath.

Patrick stares at her and shoves her over. I laugh again.

"Come on, guys," I say, laughing.

"Okay, then I forgot to mention that actually, she goes to the stage at like seven like she did today and we were there. Then she goes back to the front desk at like eight, and then at nine she goes to the washroom and then after like five minutes goes to the stage."

"Okay, so obviously we need to find out what she does when she's in the washroom," I say.

"I'll do that. You would be too noticeable with your crutches," Daisy says.

"Yeah, you're probably right," I say.

"I am," Daisy replies.

"I can be drinking water at the fountain by the stage that she runs."

"Yeah, okay, should I wait in the lobby? Then when she goes into the washroom, I could text you guys and then run over to the water fountain with Ginny," Patrick says.

"Okay. That sounds like a good plan, so let's make sure of this. Patrick, you will be in the lobby doing what?" Daisy asks.

"I could maybe be trying to call my mom to see where she is. It could be fake though, and then when she leaves to the bathroom, I could text you guys to let you know that she left her post. If anything else happens, I'll just call you and you guys will have to leave *your* posts and I will give you directions so that we could corner her in some other place. We will have to be quick though," Patrick says, looking at me.

"What? I will be quick if that happens. There is no saying that it will though."

"She's right," Daisy says, "and as soon as she leaves the bathroom, I will text you guys so that you are ready for when she comes toward the stage. Then when she leaves, I could go out after her and corner her over by you guys. Also, we will tell each other if she changes direction at any other point."

"Yeah, okay, Patrick. When we come, you will be coming from the opposite direction, hiding behind a pillar or something and pretending that this is you first time seeing me in a while."

"Okay, let me get this straight. I will be in the lobby and text you guys if she leaves or changes direction, and when she goes to the bathroom, Daisy will tell us when she leaves or if she changes direction, then Ginny will be by the water fountain for when she comes. When I come from the lobby, should I automatically go behind a pole or only when Daisy texts us?" Patrick asks.

"Go automatically because the bathroom isn't far from the stage, and then what if she walks quickly?" I say. "Also, as soon as I signal you, start walking because I will be able to see her coming and you most likely won't."

"Okay, what's the signal?" he asks.

I think about this question for a minute and then stare at my useless crutches. Maybe they aren't useless anymore. "I'll accidentally drop one of my crutches and then you will come over to help me pick them up and say hi."

"Okay, perfect!" Daisy says.

Patrick and I nod.

"Wait a second. We will each need a little map of our setup in case something goes wrong. That way we could just follow the map because, not everyone knows the maze convention center as well as you, Patrick," I say, smiling up at him.

He smiles back. OMG, I think that he flirted. Well, so did I a little bit! Oh my gosh, is this confusingly amazing!

We start to draw the little maps of the convention center and the mini lobby that is by it that she works in the morning.

Then we start to make routes for possible flaws to our mapped-out plan in case something, *anything*, goes wrong.

Chapter 23

Sardines

We head back to the convention center and see the Witch exactly where we want her. This whole set up of our plan actually reminds me of a game that I like to play in the summer. It is called sardines. It is the same type of game as hide-and-seek except there is only one hider and the rest are seekers. In other words, the Witch is the hider and Patrick, Daisy, and I are the seekers.

We all start to walk to our stations and look at each other and nod.

Patrick pulls out his phone and says to us, "I'll catch you guys later, I just have to call my mom to see when we are going to leave."

I look over my shoulder and see the Witch quickly look down to her papers or whatever.

I smile and look back to Patrick and Daisy, who nods, and I say, "Okay, we'll see you later."

"Bye," he says.

"Daisy, let's go," I say.

"Okay, one second I just got to go to the washroom," she replies just as we reach to bathroom.

"Okay, I'll meet you by the stage."

"See you," she says with a wicked grin.

-♪♪♪-

I "stroll" down the hallway with my hipster bag around my shoulder. Inside of my bag are all the key items to success.

Key items that are crucial to success in this mission:

1. My phone
    a. For cellular, text, and auditory face call usage
    b. Or in simpler terms, in case something goes wrong and I get called or get a text from Patrick or Daisy

2. My map
    a. For visual emergency purposes
    b. Or in simpler terms, in case something goes wrong and I have to take a different route than was planned (We named each of the hallways after a main street so that if something goes wrong, we can say the street names and still know what we're talking about.)

3. My wallet
    a. For the purpose of hunger or thirst
    b. Or in simpler terms, in case I start to get hungry or thirsty and decide to use one of the nearby vending machines

4. My concealer
    a. For the purpose of concealment
    b. Or in simpler terms, in case some of it starts to rub off. I wouldn't want Patrick to see dry spots and a pimple!

Lastly . . .

5. My Sharpies
   a. For the purpose of signatures
   b. Or in simpler terms, in case I see someone I know that hasn't signed my bright orange cast yet

With these simple tools, success is easy peasy, lemon squeezy!

I hurry down to the water fountain, and as soon as I get there, I get a text from Daisy that the Witch just walked into the bathroom. I don't respond because I know that Daisy is probably looking up at the Witch every three seconds. This would just make it more suspicious.

I look up and see Patrick walking down the hall toward me. I motion for him to go and pretend to be getting something at the vending machine.

He walks up to me and says, "Don't you want me to go behind the pole?"

"It looks like it is setup if you just pop out from behind it without really 'seeing' me," I say.

"You're right. . . . I'll go over by the vending machines and pretend to be getting something and then I'll walk over when you drop your crutches."

"Perfect," I say just as I get a text from Daisy that says that the Witch just left.

Patrick gets it two seconds later.

"Quick! Get over there and pull out a dollar so it looks real," I say to him, nudging him over.

"Right," he says.

"Remember, when she comes over, block her entrance to the stage."

"Okay," he says while getting out a dollar.

I pretend to bend down over the fountain while in reality I am scanning the crowd looking for her.

I spot her and drop one of my crutches, and then Patrick looks over and hurries to pick it up while looking up and seeing her.

She looks at us and turns around. *She turns around!* Going the complete opposite way than she is supposed to. She turns her head and grins at us like she knows that we are trying to trap her.

I quickly grab my phone and text Daisy. "SHE TURNED AROUND! HEADING BACK TOWARD U . . . TRY 2 SPOT HER AND THEN TELL US WHERE SHE IS SO THAT WE CAN FIND HER!"

She replies, "Kk!"

Patrick and I scramble to stand up (me taking longer than him) and hurry in the direction that the Witch went.

"Patrick, get out your map."

"Right!" he says, pulling it out of his pocket.

I call Daisy.

"Daisy, we are on the corner of Michigan and Chicago, have you found her yet?"

"Yeah, we are on Ogden approaching Kennedy."

"Okay, we will meet you at Kennedy," I say, looking at the map.

We were just at Kennedy.

"Okay, see you there."

"Bye," I say then hang up.

"Patrick, we have to turn around and meet them at Kennedy.

"Okay," he says while speed-walking back toward Kennedy.

Chapter 24

Locked

Patrick and I get to Kennedy and see Daisy walking fast after the Witch.

Patrick and I look at each other and nod. We had this planned in case something happed, like something did. Typical.

The Witch closes in looking *really* mad. I wonder why.

Patrick and I spread apart and when she is almost to us we rush in, and I stick out my crutch and she trips on it. I hop over to her.

"Oh my, are you all right? Would you like an emergency nurse?" I say, mocking her in her Southern sweetie-pie voice.

She *growls* at me. Literally. Patrick grabs her arm, and she pulls him down and punches him in the face. I gasp and grab Patrick away from her.

Daisy and I have done enough play-fighting to know what to do if someone is naughty. She looks at me and I nod frantically. Then she kicks the Witch in the back of the knee, and she falls over like a tree. Daisy rushes over to Patrick and me and we step back. The Witch stands up and looks at us. She reaches into her bag and pulls out some M&M's.

"The M&M's," I whisper.

"Oh no," Daisy says horrified.

Patrick just looks at us with an eye starting to swell up and looks back at her with a scowl.

I plug my nose as she rips off the cover, but it doesn't help. Daisy falls over as the skunk smell erupts from the package. My leg starts to throb again. I fall over and my crutches fall on top of me. Then Patrick falls next to me.

-♫♫♫-

I wake up to Daisy shaking me.

"Ginny, get up. Come on get up!"

"What?" I ask her.

Patrick is up too.

"Where are we?" he asks.

"Where is the Witch? I ask.

"I don't know," Daisy says.

We are all strapped together with a rope. I can't see my crutches anywhere. All of a sudden we hear a door slam, and the Witch appears inside of it.

"Good, you're up," she says.

"Where are we?" I ask her.

"You seriously think I am going to tell you that?" she says, laughing.

"At least tell us if we are still in the convention center."

"Fine, you are in the convention center."

"We are in that same room that you talked to your daughter in. Aren't we?"

She looks at me with a shocked expression that quickly fades. "No, you're not."

"Yes, we are."

This is where being part Mullins comes in handy. We are skilled arguers and have zero patience for lies.

"No, you're not!"

"Yes, we are. You should've seen your face when I said that we were. Now stop lying to my face and tell me the truth," I say, glaring with my face all red and eyes hard.

"All right, you are."

"Good, now you can either let us walk out of here and you can make sure that we don't tell anyone, or you can wait to let us out of here and have us tell everybody what you did to my mom, me, us, and why you did it," I say.

"You don't even if you know if you are right."

"Oh yes, I do," I pull my phone out and punch in my password with great difficulty.

I get out the Voice Memos app and press the top one.

"Ava, I swear I've done everything that I can in my power to make you win. I've put sour milk in their water, I broke into their room, I *even broke her mom's foot!*"

"Okay, but, Mom, if I don't win, I really don't want to dance anymore."

"But if you do win, which I think that you will, you will keep on dancing until you make it to Worlds."

"Mom, no!"

"Oh yes! Now, let's go and win this thing!'"

It plays and her mouth drops open while she stares at us. The recording stops and I smile.

"So are you going to let us out now or not?"

She walks over and unties us. Then she goes in the corner of the room that is dark and grabs my crutches. She hands them to me and opens the door.

Patrick, Daisy, and I walk out—or in my case, crutch out—and hurry to stage B where the hard shoe Treble Jigs are.

The Witch follows.

We finally make it to the front and I sit down next to my mom.

"Where have you been?" she asks angrily.

"We got locked in a closet by the lady at the front desk," I say, looking at her.

I was supposed to not tell her, but how could I not? What if she went ahead and did this to another dancer? What would they do?

"Wait, What!" she screams.

I point.

Chapter 25

Justice

Paige got second, Maggie got third, the Witch's daughter got first. Ironic.

It is the last day of nationals awards, and so far, all the Mullins have done very well. Abby got seventh for the U11s. She is excited to be going to Worlds. Everybody else did very well.

I am excited to be going home personally.

The Witch didn't get arrested. She just isn't allowed to come to any competitions, or feis in an Irish dancer's words.

I turn on the radio in the car and listen to it.

-♪♪♪-

"How was it?" my dad asks.

"It was fine," I say, looking at my mom.

She will tell him what happened later.

I fall onto the couch and drop my crutches on the ground.

I think about Daisy winning, Abby getting seventh, Lanie getting fifth, Alice getting second, and all the other Mullins doing well. I am glad that I went, no matter how crazy it was.

On the other hand, how crazy is my life going to be with another baby! Great.

"Ginny, Ginny, Ginny! Was it fun, did you have fun? I want to go to Oireachtas this year. Can I, Mom, can I?" asks Bella, jumping on our couch next to me. Sophia the First is turned on. Wonderful.

Then Charlie comes over and sits down next to Bella.

So cozy.

Thanks!

Lots of people have helped me throughout the making of this book. Here are some of them:

I would like to thank Ellen Wozny and Laura Jevitz for taking the time to correct and edit my book.

I would like to thank Liz Iozzo for making the cover picture.

I would like to thank Jordan Cibinski for modeling for the cover page, and her mom, Tara, for driving her.

I would like to thank my dad for making the book possible.

I would like to thank my mom and sister for giving me ideas.

Lastly, I would like to thank my dogs, Boikey and Coco, for keeping me company while I was writing.